UNSTUCK

Unstuck

*Hope for Anyone Who Feels Stuck
between the Pain of the Past
and the Promise of the Future*

Carolyn Koons

Servant Publications
Ann Arbor, Michigan

Vine Books is an imprint of Servant Publications especially
designed to serve Evangelical Christians.

Published by Servant Publications
P.O. Box 8617
Ann Arbor, Michigan 48107

Cover design by Michael Andaloro

93 94 95 96 97 10 9 8 7 6 5 4 3 2 1

Printed in the United States of America
ISBN 0-89283-790-x

Library of Congress Cataloging-in-Publication Data

Koons, Carolyn A.
    Unstuck: hope for anyone who feels stuck between the pain of
the past and the promise of the future / Carolyn Koons.
        p. cm.
    Includes bibliographical references.
    ISBN 0-89283-790-x
    1. Self-actualization (Psychology)—Religious aspects—Chris-
tianity.   2. Life-change events—Religious aspects—Christianity.
3. Christian life—1960-   I. Title.
BV4598.2.K66 1993
248.8'4—dc20   93-15640

DEDICATION

To Azusa Pacific University

The people at APU are dynamic and encouraging, and it is with these people that I have found a wonderful place to work and minister for more than thirty years. In many ways, APU and I have grown up together. To everyone from the administration to the students, I owe a debt of gratitude for the deep impressions of love, grace, kindness, and patience they have carved in my life. Through many seasons of stuckness, they have been my family, a support I cherish with feelings too deep for words.

At Azusa, I have had permission to dream, regardless of the scope. I have had permission to become uniquely individual as they have allowed me to respond to God's leading. I am forever thankful to God for the people and place that have become Azusa Pacific University—a place where I have lived, grown, and changed.

Contents

ACKNOWLEDGEMENTS

AS I LOOK BACK OVER MY LIFE, I've learned many lessons, two of which stand out significantly. First, I can't speak or write on a subject that I haven't lived through or struggled with myself.

Second, without exception, God has brought special people into my life at just the right time to give me support, to help me see myself, to listen until I could hear myself, and to encourage me when I needed it the most. These people tugged and pulled at my *stuckness* and gave me the courage to move on when I may have otherwise stayed stuck.

To Virginia Churchill

My close friend, a bundle of dynamite, she explodes with laughter. She arranges words in a way that makes them sing and lives the days of her life similarly.

I am grateful to Ginny for days and weeks of marathon conversations, when she has penetrated my heart and mind with hard questions and forced me to dig deep for the answers. We've shared times of pain, *stuckness*, and growth. Together we've changed.

To John Archer

With his command of many languages and a vocabulary bigger than *Webster's Dictionary* John has earned my sincere respect for his ability to help give words to ideas. He earned my deepest gratitude when I gave him this long, unpolished manuscript and he shined it to its present brilliance.

Jumping into this massive project was a courageous act by John and additionally he encouraged me all the way. The rereading, editing, and rewriting paid off when the pages of *Unstuck* finally got unstuck.

I am grateful to John also for his willingness to be vulnerable about his own pain as he worked through the pages of this manuscript. It was for him as well a process of growth.

To Roy M. Carlisle

My longtime editor and friend. Once again, he believed in me. He plunged headfirst into this project just as he has with my other writing ventures. He has been my biggest fan, and my hardest critic. He is a patient, insightful counselor. As with the rest of us, he too has lived through his own *stuck* issues in the pages of this book.

To all the friends at Servant Publications

I owe a special debt of gratitude to Beth Feia and Ann Spangler for their longsuffering and indomitable enthusiasm.

When a book is finally published one forgets all the labor pains but hopefully not the friends who stood by one during the gestation and delivery. I am grateful to Beth and Ann.

PART ONE

Change, Change, and More Change

Nothing endures except change.
Heraclitus (c.540-c.480 BC)

The more things change, the more they stay the same.
Alphonse Karr (1808-1890)

MIRED IN THE MUD OF LIFE—STUCK! We all find our wheels spinning before our life's journey ends, not once but many times. Those of us who live in larger cities connect more immediately to the image of the modern expressway during rush hour. Back–to–back bumpers and no exit in sight for miles. And we all know the feelings that follow close behind: frustration, discouragement, fatigue, anger. If only we had taken the other route, we moan in hindsight!

Many times, of course, there is no easy way out of our predicament. The man who gets laid off from a good job in a depressed economy stands in the unemployment line with scores of other job seekers, educated, willing to work, but unemployed. The unusually talented artist who desperately wants to spend all of her time painting ends up waiting tables just to pay the bills. The young mother who has chosen to stay home with her children often wishes she could be out and about doing anything but changing more diapers and putting another load into the wash.

Life is not a game of bridge in which we can finesse the difficult choice or unchangeable situation. But sometimes the problem isn't that we've gotten so miserably mired—it's that we stay that way even when we could find a way to move forward.

In order to thrive, we need to break free from our ruts, to get unstuck and change our ways of thinking and being.

Human beings tend toward inertia: staying stuck in a predictable routine, oblivious both to opportunities and obstacles. Rather than risk changing the way we act or think, our lives narrow to a quiet walk in a comfortable rut which offers no room to turn, much less to dance. We simply put one foot in front of the other, day after day.

In order to thrive, to experience life as a full, rich gift, I believe we need to break free from our ruts, to get unstuck and change our ways of thinking and being. No matter how old we are, no matter what our situation may be, each and every one of us can continue to change and grow. Developing that expectation is the first step toward living a more satisfying life.

Of course, not all change is good. Change merely for the sake of change can lead to disaster. Resistance to change at certain times and in certain ways can be a sound response that preserves something worth preserving. Opportunities for digging in our heels often arise when the demands of secular society come against the fundamentals of our faith. God himself sometimes asks us to keep our engine idling until he gives us the green light. But we should be careful not to remain at rest when we actually need to make a change in ourselves or in our situation.

When I have addressed this issue with audiences around the country, the response has been overwhelming. It's almost as if people want permission to get unstuck, to change, and to grow. We all have those empty spots in our lives that are aching to be filled. For some it may mean pursuing that degree they put off while raising their children or shifting careers to find work they love. For others it may mean risking the promise of a deep relationship that will touch their lives in ways they can only dimly anticipate. For so very many of us, only a new level of spiritual commitment in our walk with God will finally fill the deepest empty spot of all.

*You do have permission to
embrace change in your life.*

To judge from my life as it is today, you might assume that it was always full and rich with opportunity. Nothing could be further from the truth. My present stands in direct contrast to the emptiness that marked my past. For over thirty years now, I have been a university professor. I've scaled the heights of graduate school, even braved the waters of a theological seminary! Yet, as an eighteen-year-old high school graduate, victimized by parental neglect and wrenching moves during that phase of my schooling, I was all but illiterate. I was embarrassed to admit that I needed remedial courses just to begin a university education. It was as if I had to start over to see any possibility of a new life.

I grew up in a completely non-religious environment, where the slightest inclination to turn toward God was met with ridicule and contempt. I had little time for religion, because I was struggling for survival in an angry, abusive, often violent alcoholic home. My own life seemed headed for destruction. When I became a Christian, it was a turning point in my life that allowed my deepest void to be filled with God's love. This was a source of anger for my parents, whose own lives had never experienced that love, yet were so needful of it. They strongly resented this change in my life. Eventually, it put me at physical risk—what my father couldn't destroy by his rage, he tried to shatter by the threat of violence. I discovered that change, even positive change, can be dangerous. Often, however, there is a purpose to life that we cannot see because it lies just on the other side of that danger. To make it clear, all we have to do is stand fast in the face of fear.

Easier said than done—but that's the essence of accepting change in our lives. It's about the difficult process of rebirth. We must allow ourselves to feel the thrill of adventure rather than to be resigned to the comfort and safety of being stuck in one place. The goal is to discern contrast when we compare our present with the past—empty places made full, darkness enlightened, insight and clarity where confusion once reigned supreme.

So go ahead, make your day! You do have permission to embrace change in your life. But before you embark on your journey, I encourage you to take a look at the big picture, to gain an overview of this complex issue. Part one of this book will help you to understand the dynamics of change and to identify some characteristics about change that have meaning for everyone's life.

In taking a look at the breadth of choice we have in responding to life's junctures, this first section also challenges some traditional assumptions about the role of change in the adult phase of human development. Our formative years contain changes which can be clearly charted. Physical growth can be easily measured by watching the pencil marks for a child's height gradually inch up the doorjamb as the years go by. Developing motor skills, acquiring an education, landing that first job, even marrying and starting a family offer clear benchmarks of growth as well.

Ironically, the pace of change accelerates as we move further into adulthood while its effects become less measurable. No one educates us about the rapid and continuous changes that accompany our adult lives. Yet today, people enjoy longer, healthier lives. Many of us face added decades to explore life and its potential for meaning, creativity, and productivity. We need to be better prepared to face whatever life holds in store for each of us.

Along with many others, I have found it helpful to view life as a river upon which we travel, from birth to death. This first section of this book introduces that image and invites you to see that river as a stream of change. We tend to view life as having predictable rapids and hazards from infancy through adolescence and early adulthood, but are less willing to face any real turbulence beyond that first stretch of river. Having survived their youthful years, many people expect the rest of their lives to be relatively smooth sailing. Part one alerts you to some exhilarating white water that may lie just around the next bend!

As I've worked to hone these ideas into the book you now hold, I've found that parts of my own life have surfaced again, as if asking to be retold. My own life experience confirms my contention: at the deepest level, change means that we are discovering more of our unique identity, that we are choosing to build on strengths and transform our weaknesses, and that we are growing in our relationships with others and with God. Who could ask for more?

CHAPTER 1

The Changes We Can't Control

There is so much in our lives over which we seem to have little or no control—the family into which we were born, the way we were raised as children, the lives and choices of those nearest us, the inevitable advance of age and death. The biblical promise "We shall all be changed" sometimes sounds more like a threat than a promise!

Flora Wuellner,
Transformation: Our Fear, Our Longing

Nothing in our lives ever really remains the same. We seem always to be enmeshed in a process of change, sometimes traumatic or unexpected, sometimes welcome and refreshing. Yet we can spend much of our time working desperately hard, exhausting ourselves in an effort to get our lives better under control. We prefer everything to be neatly tucked into its proper place.

We would like to project the image that *we* at least are on top of this game of life, that somehow we've figured out the rules and know how to play it well. Then, with alarming regularity, something happens that suddenly throws everything out of kilter and sends life spinning out of control.

- We may be blindsided by an unexpected accident or illness, or perhaps confronted by an unforeseen opportunity that takes our breath away.
- We may be overwhelmed by grief over the death of someone very close to us—a spouse or child, parent or friend—or be swept up in the special exhilaration over the birth of a baby.
- We may have to undergo the incredible pain of a broken relationship or a divorce, or we may suddenly know the intense happiness of a new love.
- We may suffer through deep anxiety and fear over the loss of a job or some other financial crisis, as well as over the uncertainties of an unexpected promotion.

The landscape of life shifts purely by the passing of time, but the increasing pressures of modern-day life make it difficult to find stability anywhere we look. We wonder what happened to the American dream or even a good night's sleep. The very word "change" is so terrifying, and at the same time so challenging and attractive.

> *The landscape of life shifts purely by the passing of time, but the increasing pressures of modern-day life make it difficult to find stability anywhere we look.*

PICKING UP THE PIECES

Think about all of the opportunities in life that you feel have somehow passed you by, and now exist as shattered dreams and painful memories. Consider as well the constructive challenges that have cropped up unexpectedly, demanding their share of change from you. Perhaps you've even felt the burden and surprise of finally having to deal with emotional damage suffered in your childhood. The painful ramifications can smash against you like a tidal wave.

Have you ever felt a deep longing to change some condition in your life, but couldn't discern the first step to take, or perhaps couldn't summon the courage to take it? Have you ever felt the frustration of knowing that a new course of action was right, but were paralyzed to act for fear of the consequences? Have you ever panicked when you saw people and situations changing, and wanted things to stay just as they were? If any of these feelings sound familiar, you know how it feels to be stuck—to feel saddled with the status quo, too anxious or frightened or overwhelmed even to contemplate change, much less to act on it.

God's ever-present gift to us is the power to choose, embrace and act on change.

In contrast, we have all watched how a child changes and grows before our very eyes. Adults often feel a strange mixture of fear and sorrow at a youngster's loss of innocence, but the child—even though occasionally plagued with growing pains—typically welcomes a whole world of new experience every day. Children, unlike many adults, can see life as full of wonderful opportunities for growth and change.

"That's because a youngster's life is just beginning to unfold," you might argue. Well, guess what? So is yours! The best may be yet to come. In order to get unstuck, to be freed from that mistaken belief that you are just marking time, you need to recover the capacity to see the world with wonder, as through the eyes of a child.

This process of re-education entails discovering anew the abundant opportunity for growth and change available to each and every one of us—no matter what our age, our circumstances, our health, no matter where we've come from or what we're going through. God's ever-present gift to us is the power to choose, embrace, and act on change. This is the core meaning of being unstuck, and what I want to explore more deeply with you in the pages that follow.

You might be bored in your work and ready to give wing to some secret passion, but you're afraid to give up the security of a regular paycheck. You rationalize being stuck by saying to yourself, "I'm not educated enough, I'm not smart enough, I'm not properly trained." As your life changes, God may allow you to glimpse an open window through which you can see a new vista, a sight prepared just for you. Perhaps you'll need to take a daring step forward and open the window yourself.

Life is a mix of the old and the new, the stable and the dynamic, the changing and the changeless. The changes we experience are sometimes pluses—a new hobby, a promotion, Christian conversion. At other times the minus sign dominates—a hurricane destroys a house, illness takes a life, a wife divorces her husband, a boss fires an employee, a once functional skill becomes obsolete because of new technology.
—Elaine Dickson, *Say Yes, Say No to Change*

The need to take that step is what has inspired this book. It offers not a simple set of rules, but a collection of clues that will help you find ways to get unstuck and begin to enjoy life more, complete with all its changes. We'll seek answers to questions like these, adapted from the work of change expert Elaine Dickson:

- How do we respond when change erupts in our world?
- What are some of the factors in our lives that enable change? What works against it?
- How do we deal with the natural resistance we feel to change?
- What are the conditions which make it easier for us to change?
- How can we better manage the internal and external conflicts that change inevitably generates?
- How can we render change a more natural part of our lives?

Whenever you face these questions in your own life, rest assured that the feelings you experience are as universal as the air we breathe. Together they call our attention to the ever-present reality of change. If you sense these kinds of questions in your life, then this book is for you.

Much of what I have to share about becoming unstuck is upbeat, because I'm motivated by the inspiration and confidence of knowing God's love. I've seen it at work in my own life and in the lives of countless others, "doing infinitely more than we can ask or imagine..." (Eph 3:20). But I don't want you to think that I take this topic lightly. Change can be serious business, and responding unwisely can lead to untold tragedies. Being stuck generates pain, disappointment, and frustration in people's lives. That's why getting *un*stuck is among God's most miraculous gifts.

Being stuck, however, is hardly something that only happens to *other* people. This common human dilemma produces literally millions of sad stories—more than one for each and every one of us. We often need to discover the strength to get unstuck in the precise spot where we feel most vulnerable and fragile. Consequently, most of our stories about change begin at a point when we feel irretrievably stuck, beyond the help of God or anyone else.

---

*Being stuck is hardly something that
only happens to other people.*

Let me tell you a handful of such stories, each one involving people who became diminished and immobilized by the change and chance of life. They yearned to find a way to get unstuck, to resume living full and abundant lives. (Like most of the stories in this book, these examples are composites that weave together the real life experience of several individuals.)

THE PERFECT COUPLE

Suzie and Michael had been in love with each other since high school. While still in college, they had a storybook wedding where all agreed they were a perfect couple. After graduation, Michael took a position with a software sales company in the "Silicon Valley" region of Northern California. The booming computer market meant money quickly rolled their way. Michael and Suzie bought a comfortable home and an Alfa Romeo convertible, and settled down to enjoy the good life together.

After almost three years, something happened that changed the course of their lives. Michael experienced an intense Christian conversion, and felt that the Holy Spirit was calling him to be an ordained minister. Suzie hadn't bargained for this when they were married, but because the Christian faith was something they shared in common, she thought she could adjust. They rented out the house, loaded the Alfa Romeo with a few belongings, and spent three years on a spiritual adventure in seminary. So far, so good. This young married couple had dealt with change together and head-on.

Both were ecstatic when Michael received a call to a church in the valley community that had been their home. Hearts brimming with hope and excitement, they moved back into their old house. As children began to enlarge their family, they put the Alfa Romeo in the garage and bought a used Volvo station wagon. God was good and so was life, for a while.

For as long as she could remember, Suzie had loved Michael more than anything else. They had always found time to focus on each other—up until then anyway. Suddenly, Michael was out at church meetings three nights a week and occupied with church administration during the day. In addition to these scheduled commitments, he was always on call to minister to the needs of his congregation. Suzie lost count of the number of meals and family events that were interrupted by a need for Michael's pastoral services.

However hard he tried, Michael often couldn't seem to finish his sermon before Saturday. Too many demands competed for his time. Saturday evening usually found this young pastor closeted away in his pine-panelled study, working on the message he planned to share the next morning. To top it all off, Sunday brought no relief. For most members of the congregation, Sunday was a day of rest. For Suzie and Michael, real sabbath was a lost cause.

For the first few years, Suzie kept up a cheerful exterior. She helped Michael row against the heavy sea of his responsibilities by being the perfect "pastor's wife." She taught Sunday School, presided at the Christmas tea, and dealt with every person in the congregation gladly and graciously. Suzie sacrificed her own dreams for the kind of life Michael and the church seemed to require.

Inside, however, Suzie's smile was beginning to fade. She had come to resent this turn in their lives. She felt angry at having to share her husband with a cluster of expectations that would rival any mistress for their insistence. Even so, Suzie couldn't find a way to tell Michael how she felt. Each week, each month, each year it became that much harder.

Because she couldn't communicate her tangle of emotions, she badgered her husband to get rid of the Alfa Romeo, the perfect symbol of their carefree days. Michael couldn't understand why she felt such hostility toward a mere machine. He began to wonder if he really did love and need the car, as his wife suggested. Meanwhile, Suzie was beginning to see that pile of steel—heaped on top of the relentless demands of his ministry—as grounds for divorce.

It wasn't the sports car or even her husband's ministry that caused Suzie to argue with her husband and still fume inside. The real problem was that Michael was doing God's work and having the time of his life, while Suzie felt bound by the demands of a noble calling. It left no room for herself or time with the man she loved.

Suzie even wrestled with her dilemma at night. In troubled dreams Michael repeated the words that the boy Jesus had spoken to his mother when he was discovered in the temple at Jerusalem: "Do you not know that I must be about my Father's business?" How could she resent what God had in mind for her husband? It was as if Suzie and Michael had ridden into a box canyon, with no way out. He couldn't see it, she couldn't say it, and the result was that both of these people were stuck.

STILL STUCK

Bob saw himself as a member of a rare breed—a business executive who followed a higher calling than climbing the ladder of success. He had willingly sacrificed the fringe benefits of his education and profession in the interests of his family. His lovely wife

Nora kept a gracious home, a five-bedroom Cape Cod built on a large lot in a stable neighborhood, close to good schools. Bob's dependable, well-appointed life had earned him the respect of family and friends alike. Rarely angry with one another, this contented couple never even exchanged harsh words.

The thunderbolt hit in February, just before Bob and Nora were scheduled to set out on a weekend ski trip. A handwritten note on the hall table informed Bob that his wife had left him for another man—not a wealthier or younger man, but a middle-aged playwright!

Bob was devastated. He couldn't contain the rage and pain that welled up inside. In the weeks that followed, this pillar of propriety began to drink without discipline, something he once couldn't abide in others. He lost interest in his appearance. He missed work. In the agony of one long winter night, he even broke the TV by some violent act he couldn't even remember the next morning.

With spring came a kind of resurrection. Nora returned with an empassioned plea for forgiveness. They spent the weekend together at their cottage in the mountains in an effort to work through their differences. A thread of possibility emerged from their long conversations, which they agreed to strengthen with a counselor's help. On their last night in that mountain retreat, Bob managed to speak the most difficult sentence of his married life. "I forgive you," he said. And they prepared to start again.

Bob thought that forgiveness was simply a matter of reversing the judgment he had visited on Nora at the height of his anger. He needed to commute her sentence, so to speak, and absolve her of guilt for the hurt *he* had experienced. Bob didn't understand that real forgiveness meant taking a far more difficult journey to the source of his own shame, a journey which he still could not face.

Months passed since Nora's departure. The days were awash with the warmth of summer, but the nights were filled with the wintery dreams of rejection and loss. The simple words of forgiveness that had been uttered with so much effort had still not taken root in Bob's heart. Inside, his anger at Nora had changed very little. Deep down, where no one could see, this deeply wounded man was still stuck.

STUNTED EXPECTATIONS

Jean, who grew up in a wealthy family in the Midwest, never lacked for anything—except affirmation. Her father was a gentle tyrant who saw his role as keeping Jean safe from a cruel world. Caught up in the trappings of social class, her mother constantly left Jean with the impression that nothing, and no one, was quite good enough for her daughter.

Jean's parents reinforced their pride and social status by dressing impeccably, worshiping God with good taste, and exercising their right to drink whenever possible. Convinced that people of breeding could never have a problem with alcohol, they abused it regularly as if to make their point. They initiated Jean into the rituals of social drinking as soon as she was old enough, and then closed their eyes to her teenaged experiments with alcohol. They assumed that eventually good breeding would show.

A few hundred miles to the south in Louisiana, Jean's distant cousin Marlene grew up in relative poverty. Her father, who worked as a laborer in a sugar processing plant, was consumed with anger at the hand that life had dealt him. Her mother was raised in a school that taught her to know her place, and to guard it by doing unto others before they did it to you.

Both Marlene's parents drank to excess, in part as an anesthetic for a harsh life, in part because all their friends did the same, but most of all because they had lost the ability to stop themselves. They were powerless over alcohol, but a few drinks gave them a false sense of power. They assured Marlene that everything she wanted was too good for the likes of her. As could be expected, Marlene shut out the pain of her life by drinking, too. After a while she didn't see anything on the horizon but more pain.

Jean never married because she never found anyone that could measure up to her parents' standards. She loved someone once, but chose to let him go rather than risk her father's resistance or her mother's displeasure. In contrast, Marlene married the first man who asked her as a way to get away from home. Only afterwards did she ask herself whether or not she loved him, and even then she wasn't sure of the answer.

Jean went to college, while Marlene struggled to graduate from high school. Jean never found a satisfying career, however. Whenever she would consider a professional direction, a voice inside her would seem to say, "Now, Jean, you know that's not appropriate for a young woman of your standing. Remember who you are!" Listening to these echoes of the past kept her out of graduate school and a career. Jean became dependent on a trust fund that met her material needs, while impoverishing the deeper desires of her mind and heart.

Marlene also found it difficult either to go back to school or to settle on work. Her inner voice would tell her, "Who are you trying to fool, Marlene? You know that job's too good for someone like you! Stay at home where you belong!"

Finally, Jean would sit down, sigh, and pour herself a drink, then several more. Far to the south in Louisiana, sometimes on the same day, Marlene would be doing the same thing.

Over the years, each of these women had become resigned to a deep hollowness, a stunted sense of expectation for life. Even though that emptiness sprang from entirely opposite reasons, the results were identical. Life never seemed to change. It held no promise for either of them. Jean was too good for it, while Marlene was never good enough. Both used alcohol to dull the pain of a life scooped clean of meaning.

The tragedy was that neither of their inner voices was telling them the truth. Like everyone else, both Jean and Marlene were time and again presented with opportunities to bring change and new quality into their lives—a job, a relationship, further education. But each had become convinced that emptiness was their destiny, and it had left them both stuck.

TOO LATE TO CHANGE

Diane had always loved her father, but unfortunately neither of them had ever found a way to express it. Dad had never been a particularly affectionate man. He was the strong, silent type who prided himself on being the provider and breadwinner whose word was law. Diane and her brother grew up, married, and moved away from home. Then, only a year after Dad had retired, Mom died suddenly from a stroke. Diane's father was left alone in a house that was meant to hold a family.

For a few years, Diane and her dad kept up the fiction that nothing had changed. The house looked pretty much the same as it had when she'd lived there, but Dad had confined himself to the bedroom and kitchen since Mom's death. The rest of the house seemed frozen in time. Then her father began to weaken. His energy flagged, and he could think less and less clearly. His condition grew so severe that Diane was able to override his objections and get him to a hospital. The doctors confirmed the symptoms of Alzheimer's disease.

Diane's brother could not face the reality of his father's illness, so she found herself saddled with the whole burden of selling the house and finding a home where he could receive adequate care. She was capable enough for the task, but Diane couldn't seem to accept the transition. It felt so strange to be the provider for someone who had always insisted on taking care of her and everybody else. She always felt a flood of fear and insecurity every time she had to make a decision on her father's behalf.

Diane's pastor helped her to see that a large part of the reason that she found this shift so difficult was that she and her dad had never found a way to express their love for one another. Unfortunately, her father's disease was now so far advanced that he had lost the ability to speak and comprehend. He would just stare at visitors with no sense of recognition. Apart from an occasional groan or cry, not a single coherent word would come from his mouth.

Day after day, Diane would visit the nursing home to sit with this silent statue who had once been her stubborn, taciturn father. Seeing him frozen in the grip of Alzheimer's disease would send tears streaming down her face. "I love you, Daddy," she would say, but there would be no reply. Diane would leave the nursing home with no sense that he could hear or understand the words she most needed to share. The declaration of love that would seal their new relationship could never again be exchanged, and this fact left Diane feeling stuck and incomplete.

AREN'T THE SOLUTIONS OBVIOUS?

Suzie and Michael, Bob and Nora, Jean, Marlene, and Diane all feel anchored to an unvarying pattern of life by heavy chains that seem unbreakable. Each one drifts around a different anchor point in a tightly defined circle, each convinced that the one thing they want to be different will never change.

- Suzie feels robbed of the time she once had with Michael, but is afraid she would offend God if she asked Michael to be more available. Michael is so caught up in the routines of pastoring that he doesn't notice how it's consuming him.
- Bob needs to confront his unhealed shame and forgive his wife without condition, while Nora needs to learn that a simple resumption of her comfortable life keeps her from recognizing the hard work necessary to rebuild their broken relationship. Business cannot proceed as usual; things have substantially changed.
- Jean and Marlene are like two sides of a coin. Each lives in a state of low-grade depression and progressive addiction because their self-image has left them devoid of hope. They need to decide to find themselves, and thus be set free from the flawed images their parents provided.
- Diane needs to take to heart the prayer of serenity: to accept the things she cannot change, while changing the things she can.

From where we sit, of course, these solutions spring up easily. The key to getting unstuck appears obvious. That's because we're looking at *someone else's* life. Even though we may have a log in our own eye, we can see the bit of dust that seems to clog our neighbor's vision.

What are the issues that cry out for change in your life? Are you longing to resolve the grief, and perhaps the guilt, you feel over the death of someone close to you? Do you find yourself at a life crossroad that calls for a change of expectations—menopause, midlife, the responsibility of aging parents, a change in career or marital status? Are you seeking a church community that will allow you to grow in grace instead of reinforcing stern stereotypes of authority that have plagued you since childhood?

Resistance to change is natural.

The impetus for change comes in all shapes and sizes. Whatever your own circumstances, you will feel resistance from without and within. Resistance to change is natural. Plato once said that "what is honored in a country is cultivated there." In other words, established ideas and practices have roots that reach inside you and become part of who you are.

An old psychology text I have puts it another way: "Resistance to change is a fundamental characteristic of the human organism. The 'self' is made up of traits, attitudes, and behaviors which are so organized that the individual is relatively comfortable and adjusted to life situations. If his equilibrium is in danger of becoming disturbed, the individual resists, and fights the cause."

If you invest your energy into maintaining the status quo, you will eventually become exhausted and feel as if you're swimming upstream against the current of change. When you do decide to change, you will at times feel as if you're bucking a strong current that would carry you back to where you started. In order to hold your own against the current, you need to find ways to cooperate with change in your life.

Accepting how valuable you are to God will open your eyes to your value and worth. Only then will the outline of the path that lies ahead begin to emerge. None of us has yet exhausted our God-given potential, which makes change a fact of life. I invite you to approach the rest of your life as an adventure, with you as the explorer. Get unstuck and search for the precious opportunities to bring about change in your life and celebrate it in the lives of others. Please don't just sit there! Take whatever risk you need to take to follow God to a better life.

CHAPTER 2

The Stages
of Change

I have set before you life and death,
blessings and curses. Now choose
life so that you and your children
may live and that you may love the
Lord your God....

Deuteronomy 30:19b-20

Our daily lives revolve around
making choices. Many of
these choices may seem insignificant. For example, what should
we eat for breakfast or what should we wear to work? But even
minor choices repeated over and over again like a stuck record can
begin to wear a damaging groove in our spirits.

We may choose to remain stuck, we may choose to move forward, or we may even choose to move backward—often without
realizing the consequences of a particular choice. Being stuck and
moving backward both bring sorrow into our lives. God counsels
us in Scripture to choose life and not death, blessings and not
curses. We need to take care that the choices we make change our
lives for the better.

As we saw in the stories from the first chapter, choice and change may result from our own initiative or they may be thrust upon us, but we can be sure that this dual dynamic will come. When it does, several things can happen. Elaine Dickson defines three typical responses.

We may be led at first to *resist*, a perfectly natural way to respond to anything that threatens to upset the delicate balance of our personal apple cart. If we dig in our heels and refuse to budge even a little, we've taken resistance too far. We may be courting the paralysis of fear which can keep us stuck and immobile.

A second possible response to change is to *tolerate* it, to live in reaction to whatever life offers. As someone once said, some people "wake up every morning and wait for the world to happen to them." They see life as little more than a roll of the dice and simply resign themselves to their "lot." Their motto is "Que sera, sera"—whatever will be, will be—like soldiers who shrug off the possibility of death by admitting there just may be a bullet with their name on it.

In the last chapter, we saw Jean and Marlene play an especially tragic version of this game by anesthetizing themselves to the pain of engagement with the world through alcohol. As with resistance, tolerance is an essential attitude for living. In order to cope with life, you've got to find a way to bear it. But when tolerance becomes unconditional surrender, when life is merely something that inflicts itself on "poor, miserable me," change loses the power to help us grow. We run the risk of losing all sense of purpose.

A third response follows from healthy resistance and grows out of a resolve to tolerate the consequences of change. We can *embrace* change, giving ourselves permission to be transformed for the better. We can choose to get unstuck and "seize the day." This last response to choice can be scary, but it's what guides our hearts when we pray to God to change our lives and give our concerns for tomorrow over to him.

Whenever the sails of our lifeboat fill with the wind of change, that entire range of response is open to us: we can fight to keep our boat in place; give up and run with the wind; or steer toward the harbor God intends for us to find. It's up to us to choose.

ARE YOU AN INNOVATOR, AN ADAPTOR, OR A RESISTOR?

Over time, the choices we make shape our personalities and help to define how we relate to the world. Howard Hendricks of Dallas Seminary has studied the range of human response to change and developed a statistical picture that fits the shape of a "bell curve"—a shape like the cross-section of a bell whose edges represent the extremes of a group, and with a large dome in the middle that depicts the majority.

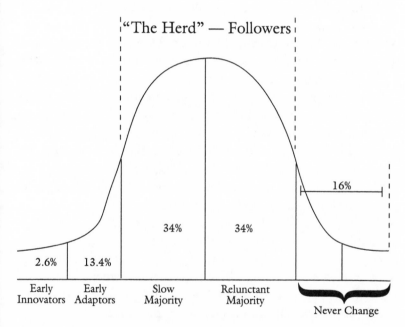

Howard Hendricks (Dallas Theological Seminary)

Your own life experience has probably indicated that some people consistently take the lead and spearhead change, while others usually prefer to follow. The world certainly needs both kinds. The bell curve for change has two halves, one for the leaders, the other for followers.

Hendricks has found that a small percentage of leaders are "early innovators," those who invite change, seek it, even cause it in their lives or in their environment. These people may not hold traditional positions of title in society, but they definitely influence the way we live. Artists, writers, pioneering scientists, social prophets, and charismatic political or religious figures all contribute to the ranks of early innovators, who represent about three percent of the population. Hendricks puts this group on the extreme left edge of his bell curve.

Next to them are the "early adaptors," the thirteen percent who respond well and quickly to change, who are willing to embrace it quickly. Early adaptors might include business entrepreneurs who read and respond to trends in the market, journalists who interpret the news of the day, managers who turn ideas into products, advertisers who market not only goods but the concepts that sell them.

Half the dome of the bell curve is occupied by what Hendricks calls the "slow majority," thirty-four percent of the population. These people will eventually come around to accept change, but are not likely to initiate it on their own. To their right are the "reluctant majority," who account for another thirty-four percent. If given enough time, these people also will accept change as a necessary evil. These are the first wave of followers, whose preference is to leave leadership to someone else.

Finally, Hendricks shows us the other extreme, which makes up a significant sixteen percent of the population. These reactionaries proclaim—often loudly—that they will *never* change. They often seek to lead society in a different direction, perhaps back to the "good old days." If the early leaders and adaptors are society's accelerator pedals, these folks represent the brakes.

Your own life experience has probably indicated that some people consistently take the lead and spearhead change, while others usually prefer to follow.

None of these categories are meant to label any one person for life, or else we would face another struggle to get unstuck. On any given day, you might find yourself comfortable with any of those labels. At some point in your life, your imagination may be seized with a completely new idea that you are anxious to communicate to others. At another time, you may be swept up in a cause or mission serving something or someone you consider fresh and original.

We all know times when it feels better to leave the driving to others, and still other moments when we just wish that things would stay the way they are, or even go back to where they were! We have also known times when resistance to change was at high tide in our hearts, when we set our jaws, folded our arms, drew the line in the sand and said, "This far, but no farther!"

Wherever you may have found yourself on the spectrum of response to change, you have been participating in a process that is as natural—and necessary—to life as breathing. I know it's not good form to end sentences with prepositions, but it helps me to think of life as a constant pattern of moving FROM to TO!

THE ARITHMETIC OF CHANGE

Change is almost a mathematical function of the pattern that begins when we feel or see a need for change and sense how it might improve our status quo. When change presses its nose against the window of your house, you may find it helpful to ask, will this change meet an existing need, or will it add to my life rather than diminish it?

Elaine Dickson has devised a little formula for helping us to understand the dynamic of change. Her formula for the "arithmetic" of change looks like this:

$$A + B + C > D = CHANGE$$

"A" stands for some level of dissatisfaction with some present condition, while "B" represents an awareness of a better alternative. "C" signifies knowledge of the first steps toward that alternative. "D" represents the perceived cost of making a change. "Who would ever build a tower without counting the cost?" Jesus once asked.

The formula then reads as follows: whenever the first three factors—dissatisfaction with a present condition, awareness of a better alternative, and a glimpse of how to get there—taken together are greater in your mind than the perceived cost of making a change, then the stage is set for change to occur.

> To improve existing conditions, it is first necessary to become aware of the "problematic" state (the general situation or what it is that needs improving); second, of the essential components of the problem; and third, of the skills and methods required to manipulate that problem condition into a better state. The same process will work while attempting to resolve the unknown conditions of a dilemma, but a cool awareness will also make it easier.
>
> —Don Koberg and Jim Bagnall,
> *The All New Universal Travel Guide*

Here's how that formula might look in real life. John was a regional insurance executive for a major company. A personable and persuasive salesman, he took pride in how his career had prospered. After just ten years, John had it all—the corner office with a view, the big desk, the private secretary, the club memberships, and the car phone. Even so this successful businessman had been restless in his job for some time.

One weekend, John drove to the ocean and sat on the beach, letting the rhythm of the waves clear his mind and help him root out the cause of his uneasiness. He concluded that he liked working with people, but disliked the manipulative sales techniques necessary to sell and write new policies. He wanted to work in an organization where a person's welfare was valued as much as the bottom line, where compassion had equal weight with commission, and where quality of life mattered more than the size of the premium on a policy. John felt more than a little stuck but wasn't sure what he could do about it, or how much success he would put at risk to satisfy his personal values.

One day, John had lunch at a burger joint with a friend from his church, a man who worked in a community-based housing project. With increasing energy, his friend described how the project utilized volunteer labor under professional guidance in order to supply affordable homes to those for whom a conventional mortgage was out of reach.

As he talked, John's friend got so excited that he waved his arm and knocked his soda into his french fries! It made a real mess, but John wished he could feel that kind of enthusiasm for his work. When his friend said—almost as an afterthought—that an administrator was needed for the project, John found himself seriously weighing the possibility of a career change. This new job wouldn't pay nearly as well as the insurance game, of course, which would require downshifting to a much simpler lifestyle, but John found to his surprise that he was willing to face all that and possibly much more.

John was not someone to act purely on impulse. He was conscientious and thorough, the kind of person who made lists. That night, he assessed on paper how his professional skills might be translated to the needs of the housing project. The result was a new resume, which John submitted through his friend that same week in hopes of being hired for the administrator's job.

When he was interviewed by the project director and others in the community, John immediately felt as if he'd known these people all his life. They offered him the job, which he eagerly accepted. With no regrets, John wholeheartedly turned toward his new life. He had dealt creatively with his dissatisfaction. When presented with an opportunity, he had sought out the first steps toward it and fearlessly counted the cost. He had gone through a process which readied him for a positive change, one that would make a real difference not only in his life but also in and for the lives of others.

LEVELS OF CHANGE

Change is like a grain of sand in the body of an oyster. You've got to be ready to live with the feeling of discomfort it creates. You can welcome change much more easily if you try to anticipate its effects upon you and upon others and to accept the consequences in advance. Our capacity to accept change depends a lot on how we see ourselves. That all-important self-concept begins to take shape very early in life; some of it is even written in our genes. Other parts of self are nurtured later, by values we absorb as we grow.

According to Elaine Dickson, there are several ways to embrace change, some of which allow us to retreat to where we were, in case it turns out that we didn't need to change after all. One of these involves simple compliance or conformance to a prescribed rule. When the speed limit changed to fifty-five miles per hour some twenty years ago, did you keep to the limit when you thought someone might be watching (like a state trooper) and then tromp on the gas when you thought the coast was clear? Now that only ten states still require you to drive at fifty-five, do you behave the same when the speed limit's at sixty or even higher?

Consider seat belts as another example of simple compliance. You know they increase your chances of surviving a serious crash, but would you wear them all the time if it weren't required by law? If not, or if your foot gets heavier on a clear highway, then you have experienced the first level of embracing change. We conform to the law but revert to our former behavior whenever an authority figure isn't there to enforce the change.

You can welcome change much more easily if you try to anticipate its effects upon you and upon others and to accept the consequences in advance.

At a deeper level, we can make changes in our lives because of the influence of others. We adjust our behavior or ideas to emulate a model—perhaps a parent, a church leader, a friend who has some trait or skill or style we admire. Sometimes the influence of others is merely superficial. We might, for example, admire the way someone does his or her hair and try to copy that particular style.

But a more complex example would be the kind of change that occurs when we become parents. Usually, we become the kind of parents that our parents were to us. They gave us a model of child-raising that we repeat. If our childhood experience was a negative one, we may adopt a style which is the exact opposite of our parents. Yet, they still influenced us and acted as models, albeit negative ones.

The deepest level of change happens when we make a behavior or attitude our own, not simply by imitating it but by modifying it so that it fits us uniquely. We have an inner commitment to that change because we value it in and of itself. This is the kind of change that results in personal growth.

An example of this deepest level of change would be the kind of growth that occurs when someone works a twelve-step program over a number of years in order to break the hold of some addiction such as drugs or alcohol. An alcoholic may begin by not drinking when someone is watching and then be influenced toward a deeper level of change by positive role models in Alcoholics Anonymous meetings. Change is finally embraced when the alcoholic no longer indulges in destructive drinking behavior even when no one is around to hold him accountable and even when role models fail. In fact, this person usually goes on to become a role model for others who want to change the same kind of behavior.

I know firsthand what it means to take risks, and to know both the price and the gift of real growth. In my life, commitment took on new meaning when God offered me a precious gift—the chance to share my life with a child I could call my own.

THE DRAMA OF CHANGE

In 1980, the year my son Tony graduated from eighth grade, I stood at the podium of Mother Lode Christian School in the California mountain community near Twain Harte, trying to halt tears of joy long enough to deliver a graduation speech. Paul Taylor, the principal, had invited me to speak at the school's combined commencement ceremony, where eighth graders were ushered into high school and high school seniors were let loose upon the world.

I was there not only to speak, but to witness Tony's graduation, a giant accomplishment that I had believed more than once would never come to pass. It was a milestone in our journey, which had begun when I chose to confront and overcome seemingly insurmountable obstacles in order to adopt this child.

Born in Mexico, Tony had been incarcerated since the age of five in a grim prison for boys, called La Granja. Even though he'd never had a trial, Tony was in prison for life. His crime? He had been falsely accused by his mother (a prostitute) and her lover of killing his eighteen-month-old baby brother. The adults in his life had seen prison as a means to rid themselves of this bright, alert, affectionate child.

I too had been an neglected child, born to brutal, alcoholic parents, never having known a gesture of parental affection that was not tainted with anger or violence. I knew how it felt for a child to be starved for care and affection. Tony had been deprived of love and hope since infancy. For him, life had been a permanent nightmare with no awakening, filled with abuse, terror, and sadness.

I discovered Tony in the mid-seventies, during a youth outreach trip I took with Azusa Pacific staff and students over Easter Break. La Granja, the prison farm, was one of our stops—two hundred and fifty boys locked up for every imaginable crime, and some impossible to imagine. When we spotted little Tony sitting on the packed dirt in the "first row" at our guitar and puppet show, the eyes of all twenty team members were drawn to this little prisoner.

When I first saw Tony, it was like seeing myself in those years when I'd been locked inside my own private prison. I couldn't leave him there to rot away physically and emotionally, and I knew that God would use me as an instrument to win Antonio's freedom. The decision to rescue him from his own private hell led to two and a half years of unbelievable difficulty, during which I seemed to be walking through a labyrinth that had no end.

First of all, I had to go to court in Mexico and win the "murder" case. Tony was proven innocent, but just before he was to be released from La Granja, the despicable prison director sold Tony into slavery. I had to search for nine months to find him again. With the help of an attorney, Lupe Puga, I worked my way through another maze of Mexican and American laws to adopt Tony. It took a governor's intervention to provide my adopted son with a birth certificate so that he could leave Mexico. Otherwise, I would have had to move to Mexico to live with him for over two years. Little did I realize that those grueling years were only the beginning of what it would take to help Tony transform the pain of his prolonged childhood nightmare in order to live a normal, healthy life.

In my book *Tony: Our Journey Together*, I told this story in detail and described both the joy and the pain of my early life with Tony. The scars of his childhood were deep, and much more than physical. It took every ounce of my resolve and love to bring hope, security, and a sense of self-respect back into this boy's life.

I couldn't have done it alone, but with the help of God and many close friends, Tony and I emerged victorious. The experience profoundly changed both of us. Tony discovered the gift of learning to love himself and others. From being a single person without children, I became a single parent who knew the deep challenge and responsibility of joining and guiding the life of another human being.

When I adopted Tony at age twelve, he was uneducated and illiterate. Naturally, he couldn't speak a word of English which made communication in his new world extremely frustrating. For some years, Tony had serious problems adjusting to school life. After a life regulated by brutal prison guards, he had an understandable mistrust of authority. As a result, the boy lashed out at people—including his new mother—in damaging, often hurtful ways. When Tony was angry with me, he knew he could always get to me by sneering, "You don't love me."

We finally turned the corner on his defiance and my helplessness in the face of it when I told him that his adoption meant a choice for me—to give up a life of freedom as a single person for the love of a child. From the beginning, I realized that I had adopted Tony not because I had to, but because I loved him.

There came a time when I needed to tell him what such love meant, in words he could understand. "You know, Tony," I said, after an ugly little incident involving a tantrum and a broken toy, "as I look back over the last couple of years, I realize I had to give up a lot for you. I used to have total freedom—I never had to come straight home from work, I could be gone most weekends, and if I wanted to visit friends or go to dinner or go shopping, I'd go. I gave up my freedom for you, but do you know what? I love you so much I'd do it all over again. If we're going to make it as mother and son, we *both* have to give. But I don't ever again want to hear you say 'You don't love me,' because I do—very, very much."

By this time Tony was crying along with me. "I love you, too Mom," he said quietly, and we hugged each other tightly, ready to continue our journey.

Some time later, friends counseled me to give Tony the opportunity to experience both a different environment and a Christian school. So it was then that I enrolled him to finish his elementary schooling at Mother Lode, which boasted of compassionate, understanding teachers who I hoped would have a transforming effect on Tony's attitude toward learning. There in the mountains, he would be close to Pastor Russell and Alva Peters of Twain Harte Community Church, who had once adopted me into their family circle and church community, and who now were acting as grandparents for Tony.

The results of those associations were wonderfully transforming for Tony. I was bursting with pride when I stood at that podium at Mother Lode School. I didn't know it, but Tony had been invited to speak, too. Looking so grownup and handsome in his new three-piece suit, he stepped to the lectern and thanked the school for all it had meant to him. Then Tony thanked me for having adopted him and brought him to the United States. "It's the greatest thing that's ever happened in my life," he said, and then he turned to face me. Tears streaming down his face, Tony threw his arms around me, and cried over and over, "Mom, I love you, I love you, I love you!"

My tears matched my son's. I brought down the house when I approached the podium and managed to choke out, through sobs of joy, "And now I'm supposed to give a graduation speech!" But I found a way to begin, by pointing that audience to the change I had invited into my life.

"God performed a beautiful miracle in both our lives and has taken us on an incredible journey," I said. "And it all started when I prayed one of the most heartfelt, sincere prayers of my life. I asked God to change my life. So I ask each of you today, have you ever asked God to change your life? I mean *really* change it! He will, and it will be worth it!"

In bringing Tony and me together, God revealed not only a different plan for Tony's life, but also a major shift for mine. I had been a single, never-married woman, who took the wild, unlikely step of adopting Tony as my son. Talk about change! Prying him from the hell of his captivity was only the first of many trials for our life together. Tony had much to learn about love and trust, and as it turned out, so did I. With commitment, determination, and God's help, we came to experience the miracle of a loving relationship. I give thanks to God for Tony—and for all these lessons—every day.

My life with Tony has also helped me to remember that almost nothing that really matters comes easily. The ups and downs of important relationships confirm for us what we already know: that the world can sometimes be a very bewildering place. Hundreds of circumstances, positive and negative, bombard us at every point in life, past and present. Sometimes it seems that we will never get to a place of peace and serenity.

Most of us were not prepared for all that we would have to deal with as adults. Sometimes we complain to no one in particular, "No one ever told me it was going to be quite like this!" If you have said something to that effect, you are not alone. I certainly had no clue about the magnitude of challenges which I would eventually face. Nor do most of us. The basic task for this generation is to learn the hard lessons about growing and changing that only our own experience can teach us.

CHAPTER **3**

A Predictable Life, What's That?

> A certain measure of our maturity
> lies in the fuller dimensions of
> acceptance, of allowing the transi-
> tions that are difficult but necessary
> to take place.
>
> **Tim Hansel,** *Choosing Joy*

I f you're like most people well
into adulthood, you probably
had no idea you'd still be struggling with sometimes tumultuous
change at this late date. But rapid change permeates the modern
world in ways that previous generations could never have imagined.

Our grandparents began to see placid farmland transformed into
bustling cities. The majority of people now live and work in this kind
of metropolis. Honeycombed networks of expressways accommo-
date a daily flood of commuters, while expanded air travel makes any
city accessible in a matter of hours. Relocation has become much
easier, whether for the purpose of taking a new job or merely for
trying out a change of scenery. The nice name for all of this is
"increased mobility," but this potential hazard has triggered a geo-
metric increase in the number of families who are hard pressed to
stay together. Family ties are often stretched to the breaking point.

The flood of technology now swells the treasury of human knowledge so fast that the deposit doubles about every five years. The world's intricately intertwined economy rides a roller coaster of inflationary peaks followed swiftly by crippling recession. Challenges and changes to established moral values seem to multiply so quickly that our ethics sometimes appear to be in free fall. People are living longer, and therefore changing their expectations of what it means to live a productive life.

> *Woman or man, no one is exempt from changing times.*

These changes press with special urgency upon the world of women as their roles in society are redefined. In some ways it still seems to be a man's world, but many professional and personal challenges we once thought to be exclusively male are now being faced and overcome by women. More women have a real choice to either enter the business world or to work within the home. Women have "cracked the glass ceiling" and risen to high-level management positions in many companies. Many women hold positions of tremendous responsibility, from doctors to lawyers to members of the presidential cabinet.

Even the church, traditionally slow to change, is redefining the role of women in ministry. Many major Protestant denominations now ordain women and every branch of Christ's church is facing such issues. Woman or man, no one is exempt from changing times. The pace of change is building speed and momentum, and we all are being carried along for the ride.

THE IMPRESSIONABLE YEARS

Although the world is rapidly changing all around us, our perspectives on change tend to be conditioned by the particular decade during which we first prepared to face the world as adults. We bring more away from high school than our senior yearbook.

As we walk those halls and learn our lessons, our experience of the world burns deeply into our memories. Society leaves an imprint on us during those especially impressionable late teen years, whether we like it or not.

We carry this imprint into adult life, and measure change by how far it moves us from that original foundation. High school reunions often cause us so much anxiety for this very reason, among many others. "Only the very rich and the very thin actually *want* to attend their school reunions," Flora Wuellner writes. "We are paradoxically afraid that we have changed, and (equally) that we *haven't*...."

In a tape entitled "What You Are Is Where You Were When," Dr. Morris Massey outlines three main periods in value systems programming. Basic personality is imprinted in the first seven years of life, modeling behavior and character from heroes and mentors occurs from about age eight to thirteen, and socialization of our values with peer groups, friends, and family is a stage that takes us to age twenty.

Family, friends, religion, education, geography, economic status, and the pressure of the media are all factors that Dr. Massey sees as significant in determining our values. To those I might add our ethnic heritage, the availability of adequate food supplies, and the prevalence of peace or war in the world.

Dr. Massey also looks at the decades of our lives chronologically, from our twenties to our eighties, and sees each decade as generating a different sense of purpose:

- preserving tradition (a concern of older adults)
- being instrumental for building the future (a concern of those in their thirties and some in their forties)
- questioning and challenging the status quo (the province of the young adult)
- synthesizing existing values (which is what teenagers and those in the early twenties must still do)

Based on his research about how value systems come to be defined, Dr. Morris Massey believes that our values are about ninety percent in place by the age of ten. I suggest that the crucial decade to consider in terms of how you relate to *change* would be the one in which you turn twenty, in part because the process that Dr. Massey suggests takes that long to complete.

When did you don that cap and gown and walk across the auditorium stage to get your high school diploma? Let's take a brief trip through time to highlight each decade in terms of the lessons we may have learned about ourselves, our lives, and change.

The suspicious decade. If you reached adulthood in the fifties, you no doubt envision bobbie socks, pleated skirts, polished chinos, or starched plaid shorts as teen uniforms of the day. In those years of postwar prosperity, America by and large "liked Ike" and was suspicious of things that spoke of change—including black leather jackets, beat poets, even Elvis.

Conformity was the watchword of this decade, and it was a considerable risk to be considered different. Churches were typically strong, solid, and growing steadily with large youth groups and active Sunday Schools. Traditional religious values of home and hearth were very much a part of the American dream that men and women nurtured during the long, dark years of World War II and now hoped to fulfill.

The angry decade. For many people, the American dream became much more difficult to realize as the next decade progressed. Perhaps your high school graduation took place in the angry decade of the sixties, when civil rights struggles, Vietnam, flower power and the Beatles turned the sedate world of the fifties upside down.

Conformity became a lost cause. Institutions of all kinds fell victim to a philosophy of "do your own thing." The sixties were an understandably shaky time for churches as well, as many young people dropped out to follow other gods. The church made an effort to step with the times, even if it meant going barefoot. Those Christians who stayed grew both in spirit and understanding.

The angry decade was strongly oriented toward youth. "Don't trust anyone over thirty," the saying went. Well, time marches on. Today, every high school graduate of the sixties is well over forty.

Change means looking for stability in life, which can feel as radical as burning a draft card or bra did thirty years ago.

The money decades. The seventies and eighties witnessed a gradual return to a materialistic set of values. By the time of the Bicentennial, we had rebelled, marched, protested, even bombed and burned, but things had not changed nearly as much as some had hoped. The late seventies saw young adults aspiring to make as much money as they could, build the biggest houses, grow the largest churches, live exclusively for the "now." Underneath was apathy, a loss of confidence in the power of change, which gave way to complacency in the eighties—the "me" decade—a relatively static period for America while the world's face radically changed.

For adults shaped by these times, change has often meant searching for spiritual value, discovering a desire to make a difference, seeking commitment in a time when everything seems designed to become obsolete. Christian community is a place to see such change at work. Larger churches have been able to provide a wide variety of ministries—to institutions, to inner cities, to intact families as well as those touched by divorce, to victims of addiction and abuse. More recently, outreach and mission have begun to flourish, as more and more believers seek the change of heart associated with caring for others instead of just one's self.

If you are over twenty-one and under seventy, you are already intimately familiar with one of these templates for change. Recall the first two decades of your own life. Can you identify specific individuals and events that have helped define your values? In doing so, you are describing the personal point of departure for your own life-journey as an adult. Take the time to recognize both landmarks and fellow travellers you are likely to meet again and again along the way.

THE PROMISE OF BLISS

As I approached my adult years, I carried in my mind images of what adult life was going to look like, how it was going to be. As a teenager growing up in the fifties, I watched shows like *Father*

Knows Best, Donna Reed, and *Ozzie and Harriet.* Those TV families all seemed pretty happy and normal, in definite contrast to what I'd experienced in my own family life. These celluloid images instilled a belief deep in my mind that once I got past this tough, often confusing, and very painful stage of my adolescence, life would surely become more enjoyable. I felt certain that adults lived on easy street compared to teenagers.

I still remember the terrific crush I had on Tim, the teenaged ranch counselor in the "Spin and Marty" series on the *Mickey Mouse Club.* Even though Tim and I would probably never meet, I was sure there was someone out there who'd make my heart beat just as fast. I was going to find Mr. Wonderful, get married, settle down, live in the cutest little house in the whole neighborhood, have two or three wonderful (no, *darling*) little children, have fun, travel, take "real" vacations, and enjoy life to its fullest—with enough money to fulfill all these fantasies in our joint bank account!

When I became a Christian during my teen years, my life turned around dramatically. I firmly believe that it was the power of God which brought the possibility for positive change into my life—not all at once of course, but step by step.

I clearly remember my conversion when I was an angry and confused high school junior. God touched my heart one evening through the simple invitation of a guest evangelist at Bethany Baptist Church in Long Beach, California. I gave my life to Christ in a simple prayer of commitment that changed my life forever. From that moment on, I knew that God loved me, Carolyn Koons, so much that he would bless my life in very unique ways.

The problem was that I had some pretty definite ideas about how God's blessing would manifest itself! I knew without a doubt not only that my life would get better and better but also just how that life would look. After all, I was God's special child. Wouldn't he fulfill his Word and instantly give me all these wonderful promises, just as I had seen them advertised on TV?

My teenaged dream of a blissful, predictable life was destined to be amended in ways I never could have anticipated. I believe this to be true for practically everyone. No one can ever be entirely prepared for what they will have to face as adults.

Stability—are you kidding? Life is more like a whirlwind! I had no idea that this growing-up stuff, this being-an-adult stage of life was not going to be at all like I'd imagined. (In fact, in the marriages and families I know with any degree of intimacy, I haven't seen a "Father Knows Best" relationship yet.)

I had no idea that I would spend so much time trying to find the reins for areas of my life that often seemed totally out of control, or else trying to loosen my grip on the reins in those areas in which I resisted change. I somehow knew that this false sense of stability held me back from truly living. "What is this life all about anyway?" I often thought. "Is this the way it is supposed to be?"

DISCOVERING THE CHANGE POINTS

An answer to those questions became clearer to me when I began working on a Ph.D. in the field of Human Development, which simply means the study of human life. Human development includes insights from all of the various disciplines of study that examine the progress of life: psychology, sociology, education, and theology. Imagine all these disciplines together in dialogue under one umbrella and you'll have a simple working definition for human development.

Sometimes it's convenient to divide human life into various stages, rather than conceive of it as a continuous, complex experience that takes place between the ages of birth through death. In studying life from conception to death, the field of human development breaks that task into manageable sections. Even within each stage, however, growth and change represent uneven terrain— replete with inclines and downslopes, mountains and plateaus, untamed rivers and gentle streams. Our journey through life is therefore marked by spurts and lulls, hairpin turns and straightaways, giant steps and lots of slow, slow, going.

Some theorists view the whole of the human story as a series of chapters or "eras" separated by relatively short and more intense periods of transition. The "eras" of adulthood are more developmental than transitional, not necessarily without difficulty but at least marked by order and relative calm. These are the times when someone could call you on the phone on any given day to ask you what's going on, and your reply would be, "Oh, not much!"

The predictability and routine of a particular era in our lives provide a zone of comfort within which to live and grow, a "white noise" which screens out the highs and lows that always surround us. We then have space to make certain key choices and to form structures within which to pursue goals and values. Such developmental periods typically last six or seven years.

Yet within these times are events referred to as *change points*, when the pace picks up momentarily and we know that we are growing and changing. I'm sure you have experienced such points in your own life. These intense change-events come rushing upon us seemingly all of a sudden, regardless of how much time we've had to anticipate their arrival. They may include graduation from college, the start of a new career, marriage, the birth of a child, or a son or daughter's departure from home. When they occur, our hearts race. We feel the tempo of change accelerate, and are hurtled through that change point at breakneck speed. When we finally slow down, we become aware that we are different, forever altered by the experience.

In addition, developmental theorists note special periods of intense transition in adult life, more often known to those who experience them as crises or "crazy times." These transitions (mercifully) are shorter than developmental stages, usually lasting four to five years. These are the times when we find ourselves asking radical questions about our lives that we wouldn't have thought (or maybe dared) to ask in a more stable period.

My friend and colleague Harold Ivan Smith calls transitions the "intersections of life," which is a good image for the range of response they demand. When you pull up to an intersection, a sign or traffic light will frequently require you to slow down or stop. You face several decisions. Do you have the right-of-way? Should you pause and allow the traffic to clear, or is it your turn to go? Should you forge straight ahead, or turn and change direction? Will your choice help you to arrive at your destination or put you on an unknown road, lost without a map to guide you?

When the road is a familiar one, the options are more clear. We act decisively because we know the intersection is coming and we're prepared for what we will do. When we're in strange territory, when there are too many intersections, or when they are badly marked, it's not always easy to decide quickly. But decide we must, whether it means going full speed ahead or putting on the brakes and waving the other traffic past.

Transitions also provide a time to reappraise existing structures and boundaries that have shaped and marked our lives. The spirit of transition is captured by these lines of a song:

> In olden days a glimpse of stocking
> was looked on as simply shocking.
> Now heaven knows, anything goes!

Have you known times when old habits, life-patterns that had stood you in good stead for years, suddenly seemed up for grabs? Then you know how it feels to be at the threshold of transition. It's as if we give ourselves permission to explore various new possibilities for change in ourselves and our world, and move toward commitment to new choices that may be crucial to the future.

TYPICAL TIMES OF TRANSITION

Developmental research has clearly identified three such transitional times. The first occurs among young adults during the "college years," aged seventeen to twenty-two. Early adulthood marks a time when difficult steps are taken towards independence. Young men and women begin seriously to explore and define values like commitment, fidelity, intimacy, integrity, as these qualities begin to influence their lives more and more strongly.

This early adult transition is also a time for testing boundaries and satisfying our curiosity in a way that is comparable only to that precarious, world-expanding age when young children first learn to walk. This time is both exciting and dangerous. There should be a sign posted above the doorway of young adulthood to catch the eye of those who already have some experience: "Wise guides needed—Apply within."

The second and best-known transition is that of midlife, which generally affects us in our forties. Many people speak of going through a "midlife crisis." About one out of every five Americans is currently approaching or just exiting this gate of transition. Beginning in 1996, the first baby boomers (those seventy-six million people born between 1946 and 1964) will arrive at the age of fifty. At least we won't be lonely.

At this point in life we look at what we've achieved and begin to reflect on its meaning, both for the present and for the future. We don't always *like* what we see. Part of the task of midlife is to discover that we can change the patterns which upset us, rather than simply resign ourselves to their consequences.

The second and best-known transition is that of midlife, which generally affects us in our forties. Many people speak of going through a "midlife crisis." About one out of every five Americans is currently approaching or just exiting this gate of transition.

Story after story reflects the bittersweet quality of this time of transition. The classic example of midlife crisis is the middle-aged married man who tries to make up for the lost romantic opportunities of his youth by pursuing intimacy with a much younger woman.

Yet this critical transition includes much more than inappropriate romantic interludes. Many men leave established careers to pursue new and risky professional adventures: insurance salesmen become writers, executives drop out of the rat race to travel the world, CPA's open restaurants.

Women often take a second look at their options as well. Many assert their independence and creativity much more strongly during this time of transition. They may try their wings in the arts or a profession rather than draw their identity solely from their husbands or their children.

Midlife can be a time when many people reassess relationships they've taken for granted, and when others decide it's finally time to face the inner pain they've ignored for so long in order to pursue external success. A lot can go right and a lot can go wrong in these critical few years. Sometimes everything seems fresh and new, and other times the past seems only to have built a reservoir of disappointment that now overflows into one's life.

Theory alone doesn't equip a person to deal with such overwhelming feelings. Despite all I knew about the subject of lifestages, my forty-fifth birthday found me more than slightly caught in a pessimistic midlife analysis. I let myself dwell on the possibility that I was past my prime and getting older. It wasn't a question of whether I wanted to keep teaching, speaking, and serving as I'd done for the past twenty-five years, but more of a lament: *What's left for me to do?*

I had begun to feel burned out, to disparage my achievements, even though it seemed to friends and colleagues that I'd accomplished enough to exhaust three people. Despite having read a library of books on adult development and midlife crisis, I felt down on myself and depressed at the thought that the greatest part of my life was over. I had to keep lecturing myself: "Carolyn, according to adult development, the greatest time of productivity and impact is ahead for you. All of these past forty-five years have been preparation and training time. Now God is going to let out all of the stops." Fortunately for me, God heard me talking to myself and gave me the grace to believe what I'd been saying!

One in four Americans today is over fifty;
by the year 2000, almost forty-five million people
in this country will be fifty-five or older.

A third transition affects those nearing the traditional age of retirement, between the ages of sixty and sixty-five. These late-adult years are a time for reflection and consolidation of experience, and planning for a life of quality in one's elder years. This part of the population is also bulging at the seams. One in four Americans today is over fifty; by the year 2000, almost forty-five million people in this country will be fifty-five or older.

For the most part, aging is not the depressing prospect it was a generation ago. More than ever before, maturing adults are active and healthy, a vital part of the work force, eager for education, prepared to live longer, and most definitely not ready for a rocking chair. They also, incidentally, control seventy-seven percent of the nation's financial assets! Since so many Americans will face this transition in the near future, it's important to know that it's nothing to dread. Midlife might well be our most productive period, but what comes afterward may well prove to be the best years of our lives.

Teresa Bloomingdale once wrote a humorous piece in which she described her experience of trying to unload a batch of home-baked brownies on some grateful senior citizen. She wanted to brighten some older person's day, but she couldn't find one at home. One was off to the Racquet Club, another to the beauty shop, a third working in the gift shop at the hospital, someone else away on vacation in China, and her husband's uncle (age seventy-nine) away on his honeymoon! "I still dread old age," she wrote, "now more than ever. I just don't think I'm up to it!"

One of the pioneers of human developmental psychology, Erik Erikson, lived into his nineties. It was he who introduced the original chart of the life cycle in 1950 for a White House conference on childhood and youth. As Erikson pointed out, each stage of life, from infancy to old age, carries its own particular psychological challenge.

In his latter years, Professor Erikson lived with his wife in a group home, where both continued to turn out books which shared the wisdom they had gained over the years. "When we [first] looked at the life cycle in our forties," he said, "we looked to old people for wisdom. At eighty, we began to look at eighty-year-olds to see who got wise and who did not. Lots of old people don't get wise, *but you don't get wise at all unless you age.*"

THE PEAK YEARS?

Even though today's psychologists show more interest in charting and exploring adult issues, conventional opinion has held that the time of greatest growth and change in a person's lifetime was the period from birth until about twenty-one or twenty-two years of age. The work of such people as Erik Erikson, Robert Havighurst, Daniel Levinson, Gail Sheehy, and Roger Gould indicate that adult life has been taken seriously by researchers.

Despite that fact, most people presume that early childhood and adolescence witness far more growth and change than do the following fifty to eighty years. For example, even though adults make for equally interesting study, literally hundreds of books have been written (and even movies produced) concerning just the first nine months of conception, gestation, and birth. They intricately describe each unique phase and stage, from the dramatic moment when egg and sperm come together until a newborn baby hollers his or her first cry.

When an infant finally emerges from the womb after nine months' residence, we marvel at the fact that a beautiful, complete human being has come into the world. Immediately, as if to justify our wonderment, this tiny baby begins to grow. Right before our eyes, from day to day, week to week, month to month, we can actually watch substantial growth and change occur.

Almost before we realize it, this new baby is one month old, noticeably more alert and expressive than just a few weeks earlier. If a relative or friend hasn't seen the baby for a few months, what is the first thing they say when they see the tyke? You guessed it: "Wow," they exclaim, "has this little one changed!" We are even more amazed at what happens in the small body and life of that baby in just one year. Before we know it, this little genius is starting the basic process of verbal communication by blurting out those long-awaited words, "Mama" and "Dada."

The next major stage of growth and change involves the development of basic motor skills. Those little bow legs first begin to crawl, then to wobble upright, and one day take that celebrated first step as the little toddler prepares to stride into the "terrible two's." At least books on child development tend to describe that stage as terrible, so most parents dread this stage, hoping that the next growth phase will replace the "two's" as quickly as possible.

Such parental hopes are seldom disappointed. We continue to be amazed at the rapid growth of early childhood. Within a couple more years, that dependent little toddler is off to school and engulfed in the educational and socialization process. The growth and change chart is now peaking off the scale as children take in preschool, elementary school, and finally enter those adolescent years of junior high and high school. The teen years bring a drive for independence, often so strong that parents would just as soon tie their teenager up in a gunny sack and lock them away for the next several years.

According to this scenario, the last opportunity for rapid human development occurs between the ages of eighteen to approximately twenty-two. For many this comprises the college years, that great American rite of passage which Hollywood has showcased as *Animal House*. Whether this stage is lived on campus, in the military, in a singles apartment, or in a young married's cottage, many see it as the last chance for a growing individual to learn anything significant. Education for change is presumed to be almost a thing of the past. From here on in, it's supposed to be... SMOOTH SAILING, BABY!

THE CALM YEARS?

Ahh, at last! The worst part, that most difficult and least stable time of our life is finally over. For all these years, growth and change spilled off the top of the chart, but no longer. Finally, what we have all anticipated for so long, that cherished image of adulthood, has finally arrived.

Until recently, most human development theory reinforced what most of us had imagined—essentially that life was going to be a whole lot easier once we were adults. We would all settle down, probably get married, have children, become involved in a career, and prepare to enjoy the substantial remainder of life. Once you reached adulthood, the theory went, you became a *responsible person*, as verified by visible signs like getting married, having children, holding down a job, and getting involved in church and community life.

I envisioned adult life as stepping into a beautiful little sailboat and setting out into a nice, placid lake with my family for an excursion of constant enjoyment—a little fishing, relaxing, resting, and gently sailing across the lake as the sun slowly and gently moved toward the horizon toward its setting, gently, when we were around eighty or ninety years old. What a wonderful, calm life!

Often, the possibilities for adult change were politely sidetracked, because this was not the stage where the action was supposed to be. After all, the worst struggles with change were behind us. No small craft warnings were expected. Educators, sociologists, and other developmental disciplines followed the lead of Piaget and continued to concentrate on children and youth, where the ferment of change was to be found and where guidance seemed most needed. With respect to change, adults, snug in their sailboats, were neglected if not entirely overlooked.

Society reflected the experts' opinions and bias. Our country's educational system was based on the assumption that the peak time for learning occurred from birth through high school and college years. The prevailing belief held that we had only that many years to cram knowledge and education into a person's mind. By the time we moved through the school desks from kindergarten through the twelfth grade, most of us had accumulated over eleven thousand hours of education. Can you believe it? How many of us feel eleven thousand hours smart?

Educators offered another reason for cramming all of our learning into those early years. They theorized that the peak of an individual's IQ had been reached at around the age of eighteen. In essence, we had only eighteen years to force-feed a person's intellect if we wanted to catch them in prime learning time. Because our emphasis on growth and learning was focused on children, the traditional educational system by and large neglected adults.

Unfortunately, the church also based its programming and ministry on the same educational and developmental theory. A strong progam with specific gradations is offered to all ages and stages of children so as to meet their unique needs. Inevitably, one of the first staff members often hired in the church is a youth minister to help adolescents through difficult times. As in general society, educational ministries in most churches give short shrift to adults. Few if any relevant classes are provided to stretch their minds and help them through their adult life passages. Many churches do not offer adult Sunday school classes or substantial adult educational programs.

By adhering to the theory that adults are already set in stone and are beyond the prime learning stage, this approach has given unconscious credence to the notion that children and youth are the exclusive hope for the future of the church. Conventional wisdom seems to suggest that adults need only a good sermon on Sunday morning and maybe (if you're a devout Baptist) a Wednesday night prayer meeting. After all, if adults are beyond their prime, what can they learn anyway?

Worse yet, much developmental theory has conspired to teach us that nothing much happens to adults. "Settle down" phrases like "acceptance of life" and "adjustment to limits" (Havighurst), even "generativity in the face of stagnation" (Erikson), pepper the professional literature. Direct and indirect messages reinforce the idea that adults don't go through further stages of significant growth. Once set in their ways, the supposition runs, adults not only don't change, they *can't* change. Again the cliche rings out: once you finally reach that stage called "being an adult," it's smooth sailing from then on.

THE IQ ASSUMPTION

It has been only over the past fifty years or so that educators, sociologists, psychologists, and human developmentalists have begun seriously to study adult life stages across the entire age range. Once these studies were begun, a whole new area of knowledge and understanding about adults began to emerge.

One of the first breakthroughs occurred back in the 1920s

when a developmental psychologist named Thorndike began to investigate assumptions about IQ theory, particularly the relation between age and intelligence. Obviously, in order to study this topic he needed to be able to observe the same group over a long period of time, in what's called a longitudinal study. Consequently, Thorndike conducted his studies on prisoners, the only subjects he knew who would stay in one place for a long period of time—literally a captive audience. His new found evidence, presented in 1927, showed that the peak of the IQ in human development was not age eighteen, but closer to age fifty-five!

Age fifty-five! We misplaced the peaking of IQ by merely a few decades. What does that have to say to adults today? For one thing most of us are primed and ready to learn, but we may not be learning. It is tragic how misinformation about our capacity to learn has caused many adults today to opt out of the educational process. Many people think that they are simply too old to learn.

Recent studies about adult growth have shown that the time of our greatest productivity, when we can expect to make our most significant contributions, begins at about age forty-five.

Have you ever wanted to go back to school and finish that degree you abandoned because marriage or children or finances or some other circumstance changed your direction for awhile? Well, you can! How about that career change that you may have talked yourself out of pursuing, because you thought you weren't smart enough to tackle the necessary education and training? Get back in the race! You can do it, and more easily than you think!

Recent studies about adult growth have shown that the time of our greatest productivity, when we can expect to make our most significant contributions, begins at about age forty-five. Contrast this with the way we often celebrate the milestone of our fortieth birthday. How many of those birthday parties have you attended where the room was decorated with black balloons or the cake adorned with black frosting and candles, where every card let the guest of honor know he or she was "over the hill"?

We have esteemed youth so much in our culture that a lot of us feel that by age forty the best time of our lives is over. In fact, it's just beginning. If we believe the doomsayers, we slowly begin to quit growing and pretty soon find ourselves stuck, mired in the stagnant mud of resignation.

We adults have been conditioned to find the thought of school intimidating. We suppose that all those college students with their peaking IQs are so smart that we could never compete in the class-room. We are fully mature individuals, but we believe that we've been out of the learning process and habit of studying so long that there's no way we could keep up. The reality is that when adults return to school—perhaps for the purpose of finishing a degree or changing careers or simply for the love of learning—they most often learn faster and easier than the younger college students. In college slang, they "cream all of their courses."

One of my most treasured moments as a faculty member at Azusa Pacific University occurred just a few years ago. One of our favorite students, a gray-haired grandmother who had come back to the university to get a bachelor's degree, took her place in line on graduation day. When her name was announced by the president, this short, electric bundle of energy, draped in black gown and hood, bounded across the stage to receive her hard-earned diploma.

The entire graduating class, together with all the faculty and administration, rose to their feet and burst into spontaneous and prolonged applause, accompanied by riotous cheers and not a few tears of joy. I found myself wiping away a few tears myself, brought on by the realization that this wonderful individual, this adult who had never accepted the theory that she was too old to learn, chose instead to continue to grow and learn and reach for all of those talents and the potential that God had given her.

This one undergraduate, at sixty-eight years of age, had had more impact on the lives of the other students and even the faculty than anyone else at the university, and we all loved her. When the cheers finally died down and it was announced from the platform that she would be returning that fall to enter the Master's program, everyone smiled. At her age? Absolutely! Everyone knew that she would probably graduate at the top of that class, too!

THE INTERIOR DRAMA

The most profound discovery from my study of human development was not that adults can continue to learn throughout their lifetime, but that we had been viewing the whole theory of human change and growth backwards! Research has begun to reveal that, as adults, we will go through far more changes than we ever did as children. Now that we've reached "our majority," we will deal with more issues, crises, situations, and opportunities for personal growth than ever before.

If we examine our personal lives for only the last year or two, and reflect on what we have been through and how different we've become, we begin to realize how much and how fast we are changing. It's just that we were not led to expect such change. Not only were we not well prepared to cope with it, we have found it difficult to even recognize how much change has occurred. We must look closely and with intention in order to do so.

The most profound discovery from my study of human development was not that adults can continue to learn throughout their lifetime, but that we had been viewing the whole theory of human change and growth backwards!

You may have gone through periods of such significant personal change that you feel like a completely different person. Even so, those around you—especially people who have no idea what you're dealing with—cannot sense how radically you've changed. Haven't you experienced times when you've wanted to shout to the world, "Don't you know who I am? I'm not the same person you once knew!"

We find it more difficult to perceive adult change precisely because much of it is more internal than external. A little child's rapid physical and intellectual growth is visible and impossible to miss. We can see that they're developing quickly. With adults, the physical change is not always dramatic. The years bring a few more wrinkles and a few more aches, but the pace of *physical* change begins to slow as we age. In contrast, the *internal* changes—to the emotions, to the intellect, to the spirit—often take place at a more rapid pace as we progress through our adult years.

This book offers us a chance to explore that reality together. Not only do we go through far more changes as adults than we did as kids, but we will continue this process of change for the rest of our lives—regardless of our age, education, and social or economic status. Smooth sailing, baby? You must be kidding. My experience of adult life tells me to expect white water, all the way!

PART TWO

Navigating the River of Life

NOW THAT WE'VE GOTTEN A FEEL for the big picture, it's time to look at how change affects the individual. To do that, we'll use the parable of life as a river journey, a rich image that has been around a long time, at least since Moses took his first trip down the Nile. People speak about being "up the creek without a paddle," "going over the falls," or "rocking the boat." Most recently, writers characterize uncertain times as an experience of living in "permanent white water."

Life itself has much in common with a river trip. We usually climb into the boat when the river is pleasant and calm, where the pace of the current is hardly a factor. We know that we'll reach our destination, sooner or later. Not having taken the trouble to chart the course, we are unaware that just around the next bend we face challenges and hazards that threaten to capsize our boat or leave us stranded on the rocks.

These trouble spots along the river of life may take the form of heartbreak from a troubled marriage, the agony of dealing with unreachable kids, or the treacherous whirlpool of financial woes that threatens to pull us under. A roaring tidal wave may symbolize emotions run rampant, so that mental serenity and balance seem all but impossible. Emotional rapids can even drown out the still, small, but clear voice of God's Spirit.

Some people feel that they've spent their whole lives navigating such dangerous water. Often, their boat is heavy and unresponsive, weighted down with the baggage of past mistakes and the consequences of wrong choices. Small wonder that being mired in the muddy riverbank seems so inviting.

We all need to paddle over to the side and rest for a while at certain times in our lives. There have been times when I've wanted to stop the world. This means I have to rest a bit, even if others still have strength or opportunity to navigate the river. I need to bail out my boat, clean out the junk, seek a little rejuvenation and warmth for myself, and maybe don a dry change of clothes before I can set forth anew.

Yet many people today have been hugging the bank of the river for a very long time, and for what they believe to be very good reasons. Exhausted and confused, they huddle at riverside and wonder how so many others seem to be able to stay afloat on the swiftly-moving waters. Perhaps they never expected to be in the river in the first place, and thought the bank was a great place to set up camp for life. Or they may be trying to discover the reason they fell out of the boat—why they have been so hurt, so bruised, so unjustly betrayed. They may not be able to let go of the security that the riverbank seems to provide.

Clutching a branch rooted in the riverbank, holding on for dear life, and nursing their bruises, these wounded navigators may hear someone else who is passing downriver call out, "Hey, come join in the fun!" The tragedy for so many who are stuck is that resignation to their fate has rendered them deaf to such voices. Fun? Their pain drowns out the very idea. While the river of life carries others to a place of greater warmth and safety, these stranded souls may no longer even see the water, only the lonely place where they huddle.

Yet the river is still flowing, and souls must flow with it. Sooner or later, the time will come to push into the center of the stream once again, despite the voices of resistance which tell us to stay by the shore. We somehow know that we won't find our whole purpose in life as long as we stay stuck. In this section of the book, we'll spend time on the river, exploring the stream, being replenished on its banks, feeling the support of the hands and voices of fellow-travellers, yet cultivating important habits to help us get unstuck and to keep moving on.

CHAPTER 4

The Unexpected Ride

We can endure, transcend, and
transform the storminess when we
see the meaning and mystery of it.

Sue Monk Kidd, *When the Heart Waits*

T hink back upon who you were
five years ago, using any stan-
dard you like. The chances are that you are a significantly different
person than you were then. In fact, look at who and where you
were only one year ago, and you will probably come to realize how
much change has come into your life in just one cycle around the
sun. There are times when life seems more mellow, and other
times when you wish you had a seatbelt, but life is not static.

*Sometimes change can feel like an earthquake, but
change is more than a series of unsettling events.*

Where does the past year of your life fit on the Richter scale?
Was it marked by shocks at the level of one or two, a time of mild
tremors, changing your landscape so subtly that you hardly
noticed? Was this the year you discovered you needed bifocals or
when your firstborn went to her very first school dance? It might
have been your birthday only a few months ago when you realized

you didn't know how to program your new VCR or answering machine or fancy new microwave. Did the company president take you aside a week or so ago to suggest gently but firmly that your hot theory of management was a little out of date?

Or did you experience a major quake—measuring a seven or higher on the Richter scale—that rocked the fault lines of your life and caused violent shifts and slippage, perhaps with such major damage that you are only just now finding the strength to rebuild? Was this the bleak winter when your spouse left you or the summer when you had to face the loss of your job and the prospect of extended unemployment? Was it just last spring that your son died? The tears you shed make you feel as if it were yesterday. You're still sorting through the pieces of your grief and just going through the motions of life.

Sometimes change can feel like an earthquake, but change is more than a series of unsettling events. I experience it as a continuous process, one that always throws us against the unexpected. I see two disillusioning constants in adult life:

1. Not finding what we expected.
2. Not expecting what we find!

Because change is both continuous and unexpected, I'm not satisfied merely with a landlocked analogy for life, where the terrain is stable and solid and where change represents an occasional jolting trauma. A more fluid image works better most of the time, which is the reason that I continue to return to the picture of a river. From the time we are born until we die, you and I negotiate the course of this river, its calm stretches, its wild rapids, its confusing currents. This river is continually on the move, sometimes flowing steadily at five miles an hour and then suddenly roiling along at fifty. No matter how hard we try to stop that river, we can't slow its progress completely. It still inevitably winds its way from the source to the sea.

Some of us try in vain to stop the river of life, to stop time or perhaps even reverse it. We may try to look younger, or spend lots of money on skin care or new clothing or a flashy car, or whatever else promises to restore our youth. But we can't stop the aging process any more than we can prevent the passage of a river. In this sense, miles and years are much the same.

From birth to death, people have no choice but to entrust the whole of their being to the caress of life's river. We do not ask to be born. We don't choose our parents, our siblings, our ethnic heritage, our social or economic status, our inner gifts. We ride the river, guided by the hand of God, even when we don't know he is there.

WE ARE ALL ADRIFT

The Bible supplies us with a vivid example of this basic lesson about life. In the second chapter of Exodus, we read about a Hebrew boy-child whose mother protects him from the wrath of Pharaoh. She first conceals him for three months, then places him in the Nile, cradled in a little basket fashioned from papyrus stalks and waterproofed with pitch.

This mother is motivated by love for her child and a desire to preserve his life, but that's almost beside the point. Moses' experience is much like our own—cast adrift on the river as an infant, launched on an arduous journey that is not of his choosing. There he floats along, observed from the bank by his sister, Miriam. When Pharaoh's daughter spies him and fishes him from the stream, she is moved by his crying and takes him into the palace to be raised as her own son. God has watched over the child by guiding the basket into accepting hands.

Miriam arranges with Pharaoh's daughter to secure a nurse for the boy, who is, of course, none other than the baby's mother. The Egyptian princess names him Moses, which in Hebrew is close to a verb which means "to draw out." That name might have been the "nurse's" suggestion. In the ancient language of Egypt the name is close to another word which means "to beget a child."

Pharaoh's daughter believed she had rescued Moses from perishing in the river. The truth was that she had only lifted him out of the Nile at the prompting of God. Moses was about to enter another river, one that was much more dangerous, with turns that would take him to the land of Midian, back to Egypt, across the Red Sea, and into the wilderness. While wandering in the desert with the Israelites, the only water he would see was a stream that gushed miraculously from a rock.

This whole saga is the river journey of greater consequence. In this journey the water was other than literal, but the destination was the promised land (which Moses would see but not enter), the chart was drawn from God's commandments, and the courage to face the journey lay in obedience to God's will and choice for his people. This is the kind of journey that we all find ourselves taking, because we, like Moses, are children of God.

White-water rafting is exhilarating because of its variety and adventure, but it also offers a strong metaphor for life itself and the changes we encounter along the way.

Some of you may have experienced a river journey not in a papyrus boat, but in an inflatable raft built to withstand the rush of white water. White-water rafting is exhilarating because of its variety and adventure, but it also offers a strong metaphor for life itself and the changes we encounter along the way.

Anyone who spends time getting to know a river discovers that there are places where the river runs wide, where the current is strong and constant yet safe and somewhat calm. These are the places where we feel confident enough to put in our raft. Even there, we feel the power and energy of the water. As we're borne along in the raft at a slower pace, we can enjoy the surrounding beauty, the fellowship with others who may be in our raft or in the one next to us, and perhaps even fish or rest a little.

Those calm waters represent times in our lives that we wish we could capture and bottle forever, when it seems like almost everything is running smoothly and life appears to be under control. We wish these times would never end, even though we know they must.

A wonderful picture hangs in the Metropolitan Museum of Art, painted in the last century by Martin Heade. It shows a man sitting on a plank with his dog, staring at a glass-smooth body of water, which might be a lake, a cove, or a meandering river. Two boats are on the water, one with a sail barely stretched from the wind, the other a rowboat. Both crafts seem to be bearing toward the shore.

At first glance, however, you think it's a restful scene. You want to sit with the man on the plank and catch your breath. Then your eyes begin to notice the subtle signs of a change in the sky and realize why the painting's title is *The Coming Storm*. The light in the picture is an eerie yellow, trapped beneath a slate-grey sky. The calm appearance of the water is about to give way to fury, and the boats are hurrying home.

THE CHURCH DOES NOT OWN BOATS

There are times when life's river rages out of control. Spurred by the weather or the river's natural current, chilling waves of cold water lash down on us, filling our raft to the point when we feel panicky. We are convinced we will sink and perhaps drown. Sudden, unexpected things begin to happen that threaten to change the whole course of our lives. Unprepared to face the rapids, we're terrified that we may never survive this passage of the river.

Often we feel isolated in this frightening experience. *Why me? After all, change shouldn't be happening to me!* Wisps of guilt arise like smoke from a drowned campfire. We are somehow led to believe that if we were truly good persons, doing all of the right things, we would still be sailing smoothly along. Those of us who are faithful churchgoers attempting to put God first in our lives can be seized by especially strong guilt. Somewhere, along a calmer stretch of water perhaps, we have come to believe that we should be exempt from challenges, problems, and difficult transitions. Tell that to Moses!

All around us every day, we see other people struggling against the current with such difficulty that it seems as if their life rafts may fall apart at any moment. Sometimes we have to resist the tendency to judge their faith rather than stand by them in the midst of their pain. Jesus chose to embrace a variety of tax collectors, sinners, and other ordinary human beings. In Matthew's Gospel, Jesus speaks to us about the authority to judge, given to him by God, but not meant for us. "Do not judge," he says, "or you too will be judged. For in the same way you judge others, you will be judged, and with the measure you use, it will be measured to you" (Mt 7:1-2).

Somewhere, along a calmer stretch of water perhaps, we have come to believe that we should be exempt from challenges, problems, and difficult transitions.

Still, many people show an all-too-human tendency to seek a convenient scapegoat for any change that causes distress and confusion in their lives. Some blame the government, some the school system, and still others blame the church. Despite the lessons history teaches us about ongoing turmoil, it's easy to assume that the church must surely have had the power in some golden age to iron out the wrinkles of life and leave us with something smooth and silky. If not then, how about now?

The famous radio storyteller Garrison Keillor used the metaphor of the river to express a related thought in a book called *We Are Still Married*. "Back then," he wrote, speaking of a time thirty years ago, "the river was wide and deep and fast and the church owned the boats. The church ferried you across to the land of bliss and you stayed there for the rest of your life with the one you went across with, or so we believed."

Whatever we may have believed, then or now, that scenario lies far from reality. There was white water in the river of life thirty, fifty, a hundred years ago, and the church never owned the boats. The church was just a collection point for the flotilla of rafts that were already on their way downstream, while those aboard trusted in God's grace to see them through. There was no land of bliss on either side of the river, even though many people wanted to believe that some combination of choices would lead them to discover such a place of refuge.

The desire for heaven on earth persists in the church to this day. How often have you heard Christians offer well-intentioned but simplistic solutions (usually to other people's problems)? *If they would just get right with God, or put God first, then their lives would get better and their problems would go away,* or so these believers intone.

Can you think of any saints, living or dead, to whom God gave such a gift? Look what happened to Jesus when he put God's will first at Gethsemane. In New Testament times, the Greek word for judgment was "krisis." God's judgment of our readiness to serve him has often taken the form of a life crisis. To choose God's way often means literally to overcome our fear of established patterns and accept the risks of uncertainty and change.

Many Christians who are in the middle of major rapids—for whom everything seems to be falling apart or away—still come to church with a big smile on their faces and pretend that everything is all right. They project the false image of smooth sailing all the way. People need to find the honesty and courage to be vulnerable, to share their pain. It's OK to say, "I'm hurting and I'm sinking." Admitting our pain enables us to seek counsel and the help we need to come through a difficult stretch of river. Once we emerge, we may discover that we ourselves are now able to counsel others when the need arises.

When the captive people of Judah cried out "by the waters of Babylon" against the trials of life in that strange land, the prophet Jeremiah sent them a letter in which he wrote down the word of God he'd received for them. God said, "...For I know the plans I have for you," declares the Lord, "plans to prosper you and not to harm you, plans to give you a hope and a future" (Jer 29:11).

He might have written that for me. In fact, I believe that he did and have made that verse a watchword for my life. I believe God gives us the power and the strength to go down our own river. He guides us, supplies a raft of grace that will carry us over the shoals and rapids, and helps us to recover our own strength in calmer waters.

We are all on this river; none of us is exempt from its rages.

Whether the rapids proved a positive or negative experience, I can't think of one person I know who has managed to get down that river without somehow getting wet, or without the feeling that his or her life was at risk of falling apart. Being a Christian does not mean that somehow we are miraculously picked up off of the river and permanently exempted from life's tragedies, problems, and uncertainties.

Admitting our pain enables us to seek counsel and the help we need to come through a difficult stretch of river. Once we emerge, we may discover that we ourselves are now able to counsel others when the need arises.

I spend most weekends traveling throughout the country to speak at churches, conferences, conventions, and retreats. The image of the river travels with me wherever I go. It reminds me that I must engage fully with life and not allow the illusion of safety to placate my fears. The Bible says that "...perfect love drives out fear..." (1 Jn 4:18). Even so, fear can inhibit our desire to love and be loved, to serve and to be served, to speak out or to listen. Fear also nibbles at our faith that life is not an accident, that we are safely harbored in the hands of our Creator.

As I teach and share, I am as honest, open, and vulnerable as I can be about the painful issues in my life that have driven me toward God, the true place of rest where I have found deep inner healing. People seem to identify readily with an honest confession that life is painfully difficult and often disappointing. It seems to give them the freedom to share their life's journey with me. I try to listen with a heart that senses the full range of their feelings because I know there is hope, help, and healing in God.

God's healing goes deep enough to free us from even inherited bondage. He is able to lift from us burdens we have carried for many years, perhaps even from birth. God helped me deal with the pain from my mother's spiteful statement that my father hated me and that one day he would kill me. I lived in fear of that day until the day my father died. I also had to live with the knowledge that he never wanted me in his life, from the first day I breathed. That fact never changed, but I came to see that each one of us is special to God, because we are created in his image. God's love is deep and wide enough to span rapids of any dimension and to give us courage to keep moving down the river.

Being a Christian does not mean that somehow we are miraculously picked up off of the river and permanently exempted from life's tragedies, problems, and uncertainties.

I've heard stories that make mine seem not so bad. Other people have told me about things that should never have happened to anyone. My heart breaks a little each time. Over the years and in my travels, I have heard thousands of versions of the white-water experience. One element in all of these stories has never failed to grieve me: when someone hits the rapids and then becomes stuck where the river rages at its worst.

THE DROWNING POOL

Most of my speaking engagements are "firsts"—First Presbyterian, First Baptist, First Nazarene, First Assembly of God. There are exceptions to the rule and some are especially exceptional. For example, I have had the opportunity to speak on several Christian cruises while sailing through the warm, crystal clear waters of the Caribbean, the beautiful Mexican Riviera, and the breathtaking inland passage of Alaska. It's a wonderful and relaxing way to take a working vacation, filled with incredible beauty, adventure, and Christian fellowship. You really expect it will be smooth sailing, and it comes as a surprise when you encounter white water. But it happens.

I will never forget one particular week-long cruise through the Caribbean on which my friend and colleague Harold Ivan Smith and I were invited to speak to one hundred fifty single adults. We usually had our sessions during the evenings or mornings so that the prime daylight hours were free for fun and activity. Having just finished my first morning presentation dealing with single adult issues, I was really looking forward to sunning on the deck.

Before I could even collect my folder of notes, a very distraught woman darted toward the podium and grabbed my arm in an angry way, even though a friend was trying to hold her back. Her hands were trembling and tears were welling up in her eyes. I had already received numerous responses to my lecture, almost all positive. Not being able to recall anything I'd said that would cause such a strong reaction, I wasn't sure what to make of this woman's intense reaction.

"What do you have to say to widows?" she cried out. "Are either you or Harold going to talk about being widowed? Nobody ever addresses the topic!" Her face was bright red and the vessels in her neck bulged as her voice quavered with anger and utter frustration. "No one cares about us. You have no idea what we're going through! Are you going to talk to us?" By now this woman was squeezing my arm so hard it hurt.

"I'm very sorry," I said, trying to calm her with an apology. "I hadn't planned on addressing that topic specifically in these general sessions and I don't think Harold is planning on doing it either. But we would both be more than willing to have a special time and meet with all of you here on the cruise who are widowed." Doing my level best to be attentive and genuinely sympathetic, I tried to offer some sort of comfort and attention.

This wounded widow wasn't really listening. She blurted out again, "No one cares, no one cares! You have no idea how painful it is to lose your husband. You have no idea what hell life has been like. It's unbearable. It's hell!" she repeated. Her friend seemed embarrassed by her behavior and tried to console her, to no avail. As if fueled by her own words, she became even more agitated and distraught. My mind raced to find just the right words to comfort her but nothing came.

I sensed that this woman was not about to give up easily on our conversation, even though the room was practically deserted. I also felt that she very much wanted to tell me what happened. I decided that the best thing to do was to just let her talk and let this anger out. I tried to put the puzzle together in my mind. I had the impression that her husband must have died recently, perhaps within the past three to six months because her pain and anger seemed so raw. Maybe her parents or close friends had put together some money to send her on this cruise in hopes that it would get her mind off her loss.

"Excuse me," I said, "but I don't know your name."

"Charlene," she replied, half under her breath.

"Charlene, do you mind telling me what happened to your husband?" I gently asked.

Charlene hardly took a breath before the words came rushing out. "He was killed in a car accident on Christmas Eve."

How tragic, I thought, as Charlene continued her story without pause. "I needed a few things at the store and so I had him go get them for me," she said. "On his way there, just a mile from our house, a car ran a red light, smashing into his car. He was killed instantly."

A picture of his fatal crash sprang into my mind with graphic clarity. Before I could offer any words of condolence, Charlene pressed on, tears streaming down her still-angry face. "It's terrible being a widow," she said "You have no idea how painful and how hard it's been."

I was hardly prepared for her next comment. "We never should have gotten married," she stated flatly.

I was taken aback. "What do you mean?" I responded. Charlene glanced at her friend, who looked at me and then lowered her head to stare at the floor.

"I never did love him. When I got pregnant, he wanted to get married. You know, give the kid a legal father.... I never should have done it. I would have been better off not getting married. We had a miserable marriage." Charlene paused a second for breath, looked me straight in the eye, and continued, "I'd finally decided to divorce the guy. I already had my bags packed that same night he was killed. I was going to leave him the next day, right after Christmas dinner. The kids could stay with him. He was always a better father than I was a mother!"

Charlene's confession was so revealing, as was her tense and angry face. Address the topic of being a widow? She wasn't dealing only with the death of her husband but with the ugliness of her own pain and guilt about what she had planned to do. She couldn't handle what was going on inside of her and it was ripping her apart.

Her friend and I both stood there speechless for a few seconds, not knowing what to say in response. This woman obviously needed professional counseling to help her resolve these issues and she needed it soon.

Finally I managed to say, "Charlene, when did this accident happen?" Rage choked her voice as she shouted, **"EIGHT YEARS AGO!"**

Eight years! Eight years of not letting go! Eight years of holding on to what had become a debilitating pain and unbelievable guilt... eight years of her life literally paralyzed... eight years of reliving over and over again the tragedy of her husband's sudden death as if it had been caused by her clandestine plans. Eight years with no professional counseling, with so much energy for life wasted. Yes, eight years of holding on to the side of the river, almost drowning, yet unable to let go of the memory, guilt, and pain that had engulfed her life.

Charlene had been stuck for all those years on the side of the river. She had clung there so long that she had literally reprogrammed her mind in order to go on living with her grief and guilt. She was drowning emotionally and psychologically. Charlene had literally checked out of life, blotted out the sight of the river. The waters kept rising around her hiding place but she had long since given up even swimming. She was barely treading water, barely keeping her head high enough to take in precious gulps of air.

People who are stuck in this way relive, rehearse, and replay the closed loop of their story year after year, as if by letting it go they would suffer the loss of an essential and valued part of themselves.

Their identity becomes entrapped in a wound or painful experience, which festers far from the core of their real selves.

Unhealed wounds can hollow us out, like a tree that dies from the inside. Yet sometimes it seems to us that if we let go of what gives us pain, then nothing will be left but an empty shell. This is the paradox that keeps us from re-entering the river, to encounter the present and live in it, to make healthy choices and liberate our God-given gifts, our true passions and desires.

*Unhealed wounds can hollow us out,
like a tree that dies from the inside.*

I respond deeply when I hear from someone who is not only stuck because of what has happened to them but who has also been paralyzed by inaction for years. These poor souls seem to be convinced that they will never get beyond their obstacle to achieve spiritual and personal well-being, so they simply cease to try. They may spend the rest of their lives literally freeze-framed at that point of tragedy and trauma, stuck by the side of the river, confused, and desperately lonely.

NOT GETTING SWAMPED

Everyone knows how it feels to be stuck from time to time. It's impossible to avoid, because it's part of being human. Who has not become hung up on a problem, or numbed by some tragedy that comes crashing unexpectedly into life, or faced uncertainty over new issues, challenges, or opportunities? The question is not whether or not we *will* get stuck but when.

The more important question is, will we find a way to float over the snag and move freely again? We've all met people who have done just that. Here is one example—a bright, energetic wife and mother I'll call Karen, who found the courage to look inside and nurture a hidden gift that opened new directions for her life.

Everyone who knew Karen considered her an ideal wife and

mother. She would have been a great role model for any family values workshop. Karen raised three children in a suburb of New York and as far as I can tell never resented a minute of it. With a strong commitment to parenthood, she would never have considered herself stuck in that responsibility, one which she undertook with joy and creativity. But when the last of her kids approached school-age, Karen began to wonder if God might have something else in mind for her time and talents. Except as a church volunteer, she had no work experience outside the home. She had yet to complete her college degree and wondered what kind of career she would be qualified to pursue.

Petite and attractive, with an imaginative wit, Karen was always the life of any party. But there was a private side to her, too. This contented wife and mother was also an insatiable reader and journal-keeper who had always possessed the inner drive and gifts to be a writer. Through a friend who happened to be a literary agent, Karen learned about an opportunity to help a noted evangelist write an intimate account of his struggle with alcohol. She had always wanted to write a book and offered her skills for this project.

When this evangelist met Karen, he was very impressed with her enthusiasm and the quality of her few writing samples. Although he was a spellbinding speaker, this man was not a writer. Karen's inexperience represented some small risk, but then he knew he wasn't exactly Scott Turow either. The evangelist readily agreed to hire this little dynamo, which resulted in a book that sold one hundred thousand copies! Her talent brought to the world the compelling story of a redeemed life, as well as launching her into a new career.

This first-time professional opportunity represented quite a change from Karen's former routine. Any writer will tell you, however, that the way to write well is to write regularly and often. Karen knew that one collaboration wouldn't be enough to ground her in the craft of writing. So after completing this first project, she took steps to insure that she'd be able to continue to practice her new-found art.

Karen soon accepted a position as an assistant with a small publishing house, doing everything and anything connected with books. Her job included editing manuscripts, creating marketing programs, and handling correspondence and research. She still set aside time to write, using the study in her home as a kind of retreat. After five years, Karen had risen to a position of leadership in the company and enjoyed the full confidence of those in the literary world. Her work had an energy, flair, and creativity that matched her personality.

It came as no surprise when a major publisher in New York eventually snatched Karen away to direct their editorial department. There she supervised publication of books, with the additional responsibility of overseeing a staff. Three years after that first book, this wife and mother had become a successful career woman, complete with a briefcase and a Hermes scarf. It was difficult to balance the demands of work with those of her family, but she managed it with the help of a large reservoir of energy and love.

It turned out, however, that the prospect of an empty nest was not the only change Karen had to confront. An ugly secret lay buried in her household, a black hole that was becoming impossible to avoid. For some years—beginning long before her literary life had emerged—her husband had been both abusive and unfaithful. It had always seemed right to stay together for the sake of the home that two parents could provide. Now things had changed, and it was past time for them to part.

Even so, the glamour of Karen's professional role and the fullness of a mother's life did not prepare her for the pain of a separation and divorce. At age forty, her identity underwent another major shift, as she became compelled to search within to discover a stronger, more independent sense of her own worth, and to reclaim those elements of herself that she had entrusted to another. It was equally important that Karen not lose sight of God; this was the time she most needed his love.

Her separation and divorce touched off strong feelings in Karen. She was awash with feelings of pain and loss, anger and betrayal. She also felt the confusion that we all experience when we are not yet certain how we should react to the unexpected way our life is settling out. But Karen didn't give up on her dream. Publishing and writing became ways of reminding herself that she was a worthwhile, creative person in the midst of a crisis that had the potential to shatter her personality. Writing in her private journal grew especially important, a point of catharsis for her pain, but also her way of staying grounded and connected with the world.

Karen had always loved everything associated with writing, but her exceptional talents had been a secret between God, her journal, and herself. Her work confirmed her desire and her talent and gave her the opportunity to open that literary treasure chest. First, with the time afforded by an empty nest and then in the face of a serious personal crisis, Karen took the risk of sharing that secret with the world. It would have been easy for her to retreat from the world, to isolate herself rather than forge ahead in a new direction. But Karen's openness and courage to what God still had in store for her gave her the tools to get unstuck.

So many things can force us to the side of the river. Our first instinct is to see our situation as a kind of retreat or resting place. Sometimes that can be true; it can be just the gift we need. But when we're really stuck, the water seems to recede from view. We face something more like the challenge of a desert experience, where the harsh elements can conquer our will and stop our journey. We feel tempted to surrender to the destructive forces of wind, sand, and heat. Yet even in the desert, life is still close by in the form of refreshing oases, full of wonderful surprises and joys and memories which counter the pain and disappointment and tragedy we all experience.

We've looked at several different versions of the unexpected ride in this chapter. We sometimes find ourselves adrift on the river like Moses, hoping someone will reach out with a helping hand. Sometimes we get caught in an unexpected storm or hit the raging white water when all of the strength we can muster goes into not capsizing. Sometimes we get washed toward the bank by some trauma which barely leaves us able to remain afloat. Sometimes we become so flooded by pain that we lose sight of the flowing river altogether.

Scrapper that I am, I've learned how to survive in the river, and how to get through most rough-water experiences without getting swamped. It's been hard work that I couldn't have possibly done without the help of God and the support of loving friends. Picturing life as a river journey has helped me to see things more clearly. In the next chapters, I'll share some aspects of that image and reflect on how they apply to your life and mine.

CHAPTER 5

The Wild Ride

Time is a sort of river of passing
events, and strong is its current.
No sooner is a thing brought to
sight than it is swept by, and
another takes its place, and this too
will be swept away.

Marcus Aurelius, *Meditations*

The life I experienced as a child
was harsh and often lonely.
Rambunctious as river rapids myself, uncontrollable as a spray of
white water, I thought I knew the river well and felt ready to conquer the world. I vividly remember taking what I needed, whenever it suited me—whether it be a bicycle from a school bike rack,
stationery and stamps from a poorly locked church, liquor from
my parents' house, or food and other treasures from a vacation
cabin. If I felt lonely, I made "friends" with anyone who would
talk to me. If I became angry, I didn't hesitate to destroy property
or to lash out at whatever seemed to block my path. Exploited,
tormented, deprived, I thought such aggressiveness was the way
to get ahead in the world.

When I encountered God during my adolescent years, he softened my heart and enabled me to feel genuine love for the first time in my life. I soon began to realize I had choices, that I didn't have to emulate my parents' desolate life or continue living as I had. Enormous excitement sprang from my new relationship with God, who had—so it seemed to me—rescued me from plunging headlong over the falls. Now I was midstream, moving fast, enjoying my life.

As I moved through college and into adult life, my expectations for a smooth sail and a blissful course flowed from my confidence that God would protect me from any and all harm. I was surprised to discover that rapids were part of the adult stretch of the river, too. Some were wonderful, truly exhilarating, while others were at least as treacherous as any I'd encountered in childhood.

And it wasn't just me! My friends and acquaintances all seemed to have entered adulthood with expectations as skewed toward smooth sailing as mine were. Why didn't anyone tell us it was going to be a rough ride? I resolved to work through disappointments and disillusionment, to be accountable to myself for myself, and to make peace with my destiny by trusting in God. If I hadn't, I might well be stuck at the side of the river at this very minute, going nowhere.

One of the most common and naive sentences in the English language is perhaps the following: "If I can just get through this problem, then everything will be all right." There comes a time, and it may well be the birth of maturity, when we realize that once we get through our present problem there will be another one, slightly larger and a little more intense, waiting to take its place. Problems are the litmus paper of the human story. How we respond to them may well be a measure of our health.

—Tim Hansel, *Choosing Joy*

My varied ride down the river has taught me many things. I breathe a sigh of relief when the river is good to me, when it takes me without a murmur where I want to go, at a pace I can handle. Suddenly and often, I find myself racing downstream, with white water all around, desperately searching for a paddle or a rudder. I was dry just a moment ago, but now I'm soaked. I was on top, but now my raft is sinking. I was breathing easily; now I'm in danger of drowning. To put it briefly, I often feel overwhelmed.

This confession might offend a pious few, but whether Christians or not, we are all human and all of us feel out of control at times. And I don't know anyone who likes that feeling. Whenever and wherever I speak during the course of a year, I make hundreds of new friends who share with me their vivid feelings along the journey. They talk about the times they too have felt overwhelmed, as if they were drowning in guilt, pain, and shame. They confide in me also about the most difficult changes to accept in their lives, ironically the ones where they had no choice.

> *This confession might offend a pious few,*
> *but whether Christians or not, we are all human*
> *and all of us feel out of control at times.*

I'm sure you have felt at times that life is doing you, rather than the other way around. Sudden illness, a painful divorce, the loss of a job, even the ordinary American phenomenon of a lean paycheck and a fat mortgage, can all conspire to create such a feeling. Sometimes the changes we face are more subtle. A deepening addiction or an abusive relationship can erode your values and standards gradually, until unwelcome changes take hold and quietly mold us into people we never planned to be.

When changes aren't a matter of choice, we tend to get stuck—in an apparently hopeless situation, an unhealthy or outmoded lifestyle, a sterile relationship, or a life-sapping job. When we become stuck, we also tend to want to stay that way. Why? The answers are as many as the number of people stuck on the side of the river, and only God knows them all.

Fear of change heads the list of reasons I've come to know, but there are others. Contrary to some popular wisdom, people can and do remember their pain, and don't want to be hurt again. It may seem preferable to remain where the surroundings are familiar, or at least where the level of anguish is predictable. Some folks worry whether change will damage important relationships, and tear an often delicate network of family and friends.

Sometimes being stuck wears a more benign expression—a simple lack of a dream, a kind of placid inability to see what lies on the horizon. It's also possible to surrender to inertia, and believe that it will take too much energy to change. Finally, we can gain an identity from being stuck that may afford us the attention from others we've felt was lacking—helplessness may not make you a star, but it can help to make you a minor celebrity!

To every one of us who clings to the bank, whether out of momentary fatigue or abiding fear, the river still beckons to us as the only way to move on in life. But it takes courage to heed the call. Let me share with you two significant stories from my own life about actual encounters with the power of the river, and some thoughts about the invaluable life-lessons they taught me.

If you've never been on a rafting adventure or experienced the thrill of white water before, don't worry. By the time you've finished reading this chapter, you'll *feel* like you have! If you're a seasoned river traveller, you'll know firsthand the descriptions, sensations, and emotions the river can give. Either way, take the opportunity here to reflect on life's journey and what it means to stay afloat in troubled waters.

TAKING THE RISK

Each year in May, I take some students from Azusa Pacific University on various outdoor adventures—biking, backpacking, sailing, rock climbing, and rafting. For this last activity, the Kings River near Fresno is always a favorite. The two-hour trip from the dam winds down through tranquil woods and ends at a spacious, grassy campsite. The river-run offers adventure enough for novice raft-trippers—successions of white-water stretches that would tug at the raft and wash enough water into it to keep both paddlers and bailers on their toes.

On one particular trip, the fun almost turned into tragedy. We took a foolhardy chance and attempted to shoot the rapids of the upper canyon after they had been swollen by spring rains. What had been billed as a mildly exciting rafting adventure on the lower rapids became an experience of pure terror as we tried to negotiate a stretch of white water roaring untamed through a sheer canyon.

As we moved closer to the mouth of the canyon in our four-person rafts, I noticed that the twenty-person professional rafts had been pulled up along the banks. "Business must be slow," I thought, with the kind of naïveté that's gotten me into trouble before! This time was no exception. When we hit the canyon run, as you might expect, our raft was thrown around like a barrel in Niagara Falls. "Haystacks" of treacherous water shot anything that floated many feet into the air, only to plunge them into "pot-holes" that could draw a helpless raft down toward the bottom with jackhammer force. The river frothed and roared savagely, tossing and twisting itself like a devilish, watery rope, with waves that crested thirteen feet higher than normal.

My job, along with my student raftmate Kathy, was to keep the nose up by pulling as hard as we could on ropes attached to the bow. Maybe it was the panic that gave our muscles extra strength, but we pulled so hard we capsized the raft, nose over teakettle!

We all struggled to keep from swallowing water while Michael and Jim, the other half of our little crew of four, desperately grabbed at rocks to secure a handhold. Boat and bodies were pommeled by the water and the rocks before they finally found a place to hang on. We found ourselves stranded on a narrow ledge, imprisoned by sheer canyon walls, terrified, and unwilling to admit that the only way out of our predicament was to turn and face that boiling river once again.

Frozen by panic as well as the cold water, Kathy began to cry uncontrollably. "I'm not getting back in that river," she gasped between sobs. "I'm not getting on that raft again! You can't make me!" You could practically touch her fear. I was afraid too, but I was trying to be brave so that Kathy wouldn't panic altogether. Quite aside from the danger to myself, I was battling visions of impending tragedy—of parents, administration, and the whole world coming down on me because of my decision to ride that raging river. I prayed silently, "God, please protect us. Keep us calm, Lord, and keep *me* calm. I know you have a way for us out of this, so show us that way. Take us one step at a time."

The prayer did help to calm me, but we still had cause for worry. We decided to rest a while so that Kathy could calm down and we could all get our wits about us. None of us was eager to get back into the river. Sullen and green, the water roared just a few feet away, lashing at us as if it wanted to scrape us off of the tiny refuge of rock to which we clung.

With no exits other than the river itself or an impossible climb one hundred fifty feet straight up a sheer canyon wall, we were stuck and scared. An hour and a half passed and we were still stranded on the ledge. Soon it would get dark; no way could we stay there all night. The remainder of my class had made it through the rapids and now stood on the canyon ridge above us. They were very concerned and periodically yelled an instruction down to us, but the roar of the river drowned out their messages. Finally, all twenty-six of them lined up and started yelling in unison. At last their words pierced through the roar. I'll never forget them. They yelled in unison again and again. "YOU'VE GOT TO GET BACK INTO THE RIVER TO GET OUT OF THE CANYON!"

By then we knew they were absolutely right. The cliff was impossibly steep, the ledge was too small, and darkness was starting to descend. The only way we were going to get to safety was to get back into that raging river. We had to re-enter the same roaring water that had absolutely terrified us. We had to approach the same overpowering giant that every instinct told us to flee.

Eventually, the three of us were able to put together enough encouraging words to convince both Kathy and ourselves that we had to brave the river again. Kathy and I resumed our position in the front of the raft while our two male companions maneuvered us off our ledge of temporary safety right into the mouth of our devouring enemy, the river.

Once in the water, we shot down its current with unbelievable speed, holding on for dear life. I remember lunging straight for a wall of rocks, but the current bounced our raft off of them like a boomerang; thus we avoided a fatal crash. Finally, the canyon wall and powerful river widened ever so slightly, just enough to allow Michael, our guide, to get a firm grip on some rocks along the bank. I could see a group of guys from the class slide down the ravine. They scrambled toward us and secured our raft before Michael lost that precarious handhold. We were dragged out of the current—cold, exhausted, wet, relieved, but safe at last.

We are pushed back onto our own inner resources and our survival skills in the wild place. At those times, we need to remember the following:

I am me and I am acceptable to God.
I do not need to feel guilty for being in this place.
I can and will make it.
I can learn and grow from this experience.
I am thankful to be alive.

—J. Bill Ratcliff, *When You Are Facing Change*

As we settled down at our campsite that night, I thought about the deeper meaning of our near catastrophe. I rehearsed the details over and over—the textures of the river, the voices of my class urging us to get back into the river, the fear I felt in concert with Kathy's panic. There was no point in pretending. I had been scared to death to enter those rapids again. Doing so was a supremely difficult decision for all four of us, because every voice inside us screamed to stay on the ledge that promised temporary safety. Had we chosen to focus on the ledge, who knows what would have happened. We weren't going to drown there, but we'd never be truly safe either.

We had only two choices: the river or the canyon wall—and the wall wasn't really an alternative. We had to choose the river if we wanted to get unstuck. Even though the wrong choice was to remain where we were, I longed for any other option. I wanted to jump to some safe dry place, *anywhere* but the river. The white water represented a cold, dangerous, terrifying choice—but it was the *only* choice.

Our experience taught us a lesson about rafting, but it also provided an axiom for life. If we want to enjoy the challenges that rise suddenly in the course of our lives, we have to learn to overcome our fear and take the risk to confront those challenges, creatively and courageously.

Whenever we are faced with the awful dilemma of remaining stuck or making the seemingly irrational effort to get unstuck and brave the raging river, nothing blameworthy is involved. God isn't punishing us. We're just living in the real world, where it definitely is not always smooth sailing. We need to recognize the rough spots in our adult lives for what they are and accept the fact that life often calls upon us to make the hard choice. Only then can we face our fears and master change.

If we want to enjoy the challenges that rise suddenly in the course of our lives, we have to learn to overcome our fear and take the risk to confront those challenges, creatively and courageously.

FACING THE FEAR

My friend and former seminary professor Norm Wright is a prolific author and first-rate marriage and family counselor. He also happens to have a fishing addiction which all his friends help him to feed. I had reflected upon my positive rafting experiences quite a few times with Norm. He'd caught my excitement and thought it would be fun to spend part of his vacation rafting the Snake River out of Jackson Hole. Some time after the Kings River trip, he and his wife, Joyce, had invited me along with several other friends to the Grand Teton mountains in Wyoming for a week of rafting and fishing.

By this time my memory focused on all the fun of that trip on the Kings River and suppressed all the terror. At least in my own mind, I'd become a "pro" who knew the lingo of the river: I'd seen the "black holes" of water called potholes that pulled white water (and everything on it) down into the river like some bathtub drain gone mad. I'd ridden the "haystacks," those roiling walls of water that shoot upward from the potholes. Having pulled too hard on the raft's ropes at the Kings River, I knew just how much force to exert to keep the craft's nose up without capsizing it. I'd heard the ominous rumble of white water while floating in a place of relative calm and had felt the effort of furiously paddling to keep a bucking raft on course. I thought I'd learned enough from my own rafting history not to court disaster again.

Laden with luggage, I flew to Wyoming to rendezvous with my friends. On the day set aside for rafting, Norm suggested that we park the cars on the side of the river next to a convenient bridge, walk upriver a couple of hours, and launch the rafts for a leisurely downstream ride to our cars.

We had no idea what we'd find between these two points. The local forestry station had maps to the river—which we didn't bother to pick up. Professional rafting companies were located nearby—which we didn't consult. There were even river guides for hire. We didn't hire one. All we'd have to do, we thought, is to look up every time we crossed under a bridge to see if that was the one under which our cars were parked. *We were about to receive a lesson about how the unexpected can complicate our lives.*

We parked our pickup vehicle next to the bridge, shoehorned ourselves into the remaining cars, and drove well upriver until we found a comfortable place to enter the water. We inflated the two six-person rafts I had borrowed for our trip and loaded them with food and the requisite fishing equipment. On the Kings River venture, an experienced rafting guide named Michael Anthony had helped us over the rough spots. This time our party had to be content with brief instructions in the basics of river-rafting from me—the "pro!"

We ventured out into the Snake River, where the current ran wide, strong, and clear. The scenery was breathtaking. My raft held me, Phil, his wife Kathy, and his mom. A six-foot-four inch giant of a man named Marv and his wife, Rita, had joined Norm and Joyce in their yellow rubber vessel. Norm and the rest of us cast our fishing lines into the cold mountain water and settled in for a fun ride downstream.

None of the initial series of rapids were strong enough to cause us any alarm. My senses were all but overwhelmed with the smell of the fresh air and trees. The sound of the water lapping at the gunwales of our rafts merged with the rustling of the wind through the trees. The sun gently shone on us, never so hot as to make us uncomfortable.

The only mild inconvenience was that as we fished and ate, and carried on wonderful conversations, our rafts had a tendency to drift apart. To remedy this, Norm had another creative idea, worthy of Indiana Jones! Before we knew it, he had taken a fairly large rope and deftly tied the two rafts together. We would later come to regret this move, but for a time had become one big happy family floating down the Snake River.

After a good forty-five minutes of relaxation and not even the slightest nibble of a fish on any of our lines, I sensed the current getting stronger and exerting an unusually fierce tug on our raft. Norm's eye caught mine as he felt the same sensation. I was facing aft, but I looked over my shoulder to see a sharp bend in the river and what appeared to be white-caps leading into it.

As if an unseen foot had hit the gas, our rope-bound rafts suddenly lunged forward. Marv yelled for everyone to reel in their fishing lines. Within seconds we found ourselves caught in a much swifter current. Worse yet, the current began to divide into two directions and pull our rafts in opposite directions against the restraining ropes. Our raft struggled to go down the left side of the current while Norm's raft caught the opposing current and tried to dart toward the right of the river.

Waves shot into our raft, drenching our clothing and equipment. We all rushed to reposition ourselves; some grabbed for paddles and the rest tried to protect the tangle of equipment. No more sightseeing—this was a red alert, dial 911, we're-going-to-die-right-now kind of moment!

As we began to round the bend I saw a familiar scene. Sitting along the riverbank and safely secured were two large, professional rafts. I remembered when I'd first viewed that sight as we prepared to descend the upper canyon of the Kings River the previous spring, when I had thought in all innocence it was because business was slow. Now I realized it meant that the *professionals* were unwilling to brave the river!

It was clear that danger lay just ahead, for not only were the professional rafts tied to the riverbank, but (clue number two) they were still loaded with people, wrapped in life jackets. People on the bank were actually aiming cameras at us—candid shots of foolhardy rafters for the folks back home.

We had no choice but to surrender to the river's current. We swiftly rounded the riverbend. There, straight in front of us, the water shot into the air, generating a vortex in the middle of the river into which the whole river seemed to disappear... only to spout up again like a watery rampart. Suddenly, the gentle progress of our raft had turned into as terrifying a ride as you'll find at any carnival. To add to our panic, a huge, fallen tree appeared smack in front of us, lodged right in the middle of the river, with its sharp branches pointed directly at our fragile rubber boats.

Remember, I was the only one in the group who had done any serious rafting. I had also brought all of the rafting equipment and was responsible for its safety. Fearing disaster, I decided to take charge. As each of us scrambled for our paddles and positioned ourselves on our respective rafts, I yelled out instructions. "Paddle left." That would swing both of our rafts into one current making them easier to navigate.

I should have checked my credibility with the whole group, because I suddenly heard Norm yell, "Paddle right." In the ensuing confusion, each group simultaneously paddled furiously in different directions as we did a tug-o'-war down the Snake River.

By now our rope-bound rafts were being tossed around at the mercy of the current. The pothole loomed dangerously ahead.

Norm frantically reached into his pack and drew out his ten-inch fishing knife. Lunging toward the middle of our rafts, knife disconcertingly poised in the air over his head, he set off in my mind a flashback to the movie "Psycho" when another Norman—Anthony Perkins, in the role of the eerie murderer—slashes through the shower curtain to stab Janet Leigh.

Norm yelled, "I'm cutting the ropes!" just as his knife came straight down toward us. I screamed, "Don't hit the rafts!" but it was too late. Norm's knife skimmed the ropes and sliced through the rubber. I heard a noise like "POW!" as air blasted out of our raft. Norm continued to saw at the ropes and but it was too late.

Our raft shot into the hungry mouth of that awesome pothole and was captured by the tree. I was the first one to be splayed against the tree—a crucifixion of sorts—all the while holding onto our rapidly deflating raft. Three others were soon pinned against me. Then Norm and Joyce's raft with all of its contents joined the ungainly mass. I found myself buried at the bottom with the river's engorged current rushing over us.

Unable to move with all the weight on me, I gasped for air and attempted to keep my head above water. Amidst groans and screams I could also see out of the corner of my eye that one of the professional raft groups had quickly untied their raft and were putting out from the safety of the shore in hopes of pulling off a rescue. Again, too late! The combination of all that weight was too much for the fallen tree to bear. The branch against my back snapped and I was plunged into the freezing current. Still holding onto our now deflated raft, I was immediately followed by Marv and Rita, then the flotsam of our fishing equipment and supplies.

The three of us had become unwilling prisoners of the river. Fortunately, only a few hundred feet downstream, the river widened a bit and the current slowed. We managed to swim over to the side and grab branches that kept us from being whisked further downstream. I was still half-submerged in the water and holding onto this fully-deflated piece of yellow rubber, almost too exhausted and paralyzed by cold to crawl up onto the bank. But we made it, even though we looked like three frozen, wet mackerels draped on the shore.

Norm's group, with their intact raft, was still clinging to the jagged tree at the river's center when the professional raft pulled alongside. In rapid sequence, the able crew grabbed all four of the stranded survivors and transferred them to the larger raft. The rescue team quickly tied the smaller raft to theirs and threw warm blankets onto Norm and Joyce. Then they broke free from the tree and safely shot downstream. The huge raft looked like a lumbering vessel against the swiftness of the current, but it was not tossed around nearly as easily as our much smaller rafts had been.

Help is on the way, I silently rejoiced. *Within minutes I'll be out of this ice chest with one of those blankets wrapped around me.* I couldn't think of anything else but getting safe and warm. Then I noticed that no one in the large raft seemed to be making any effort to maneuver our way. Instead, they stayed squarely in the center of the river.

I clung to the bank, shaking with cold and shocked with indignation as the vessel stolidly passed us by and started around the bend. I saw Norm sitting up in the raft with his back to us. He managed to turn his head around barely enough to make eye contact and called out (rather weakly, I thought), "See you at the car!"

As I lay stranded by the freezing river, I couldn't believe my ears! Their raft careened gently downstream, around the bend, and out of sight. My mind raced frantically. *My friend! My teacher! My hero? He left us! Didn't he care? What were we going to do? How were we going to get out of here? Who knew where or how far the car was?*

Our raft was worthless for further navigation but I was determined to hold onto it as evidence of our mishap. We dragged the slashed raft and ourselves well over a mile through the woods to the highway. I would have lugged it a hundred miles more, just so that I could show it to everyone and say, "Look at this raft. My kind friend Norman harpooned it with his fishing knife and left us by the side of the river to die!" At long last, the driver of a pickup truck took us back to the bridge and our car.

What a joyride this had turned out to be! When Norm and his party passed down the river in safety with warm blankets wrapped around their shivering bodies, I was shocked that we had been left by the side of the river. Shock gave way to disbelief. Then I was TICKED! I felt as if my friend had deserted us. My anger toward Norm didn't last. It wasn't his fault that the professional rafters had picked him up. Anyway, our friendship was stronger than those fleeting feelings.

FINDING THE PACE

Like many such stories, my ride on the Snake River echoes the way most of us start our journeys into adult life. Somehow, somewhere, at a spot where it seems wide and calm, we set sail into life, unsure of what lies ahead and therefore unprepared for it. We know only that sooner or later we will cross the finish line. The smooth cruise that meanders along the river's shady coves and drifts into sparkling inlets represents the almost fairy tale magic of good times.

Then in the blink of an eye, life can change. Its once gentle arms grip us roughly; its gurgling lullaby becomes an angry roar. For adults out on a light excursion, the unexpected often holds no edge of panic. Because we've been conditioned to believe that there's nothing out of the ordinary coming our way, the river looks easy enough to navigate from where we sit.

A friend of mine was introduced to the unexpected by an eerie coincidence. On the very day when the loan closed on the house that he and his wife had bought (the one that was to secure their financial stability), it so happend that a major earthquake hit on a fault line that ran right through their neighborhood. Their investment lost thousands of dollars in the space of about ninety seconds!

Over a century ago, a great English statesman observed that "what we anticipate seldom occurs. What we least expect, generally happens." In your own life, how often has the pace of life abruptly changed or your routine been disrupted by the unexpected loss of job, a breathtaking plunge in the investment market, or a sudden shift of relationships when a pivotal member of your family dies? You may be holding on by your fingernails, barely hoping to survive your sudden shift in fortune.

But what happens when someone you know passes by and barely acknowledges your plight? You feel anger, frustration, even a sense of rejection or betrayal. It's important to remember that life proceeds at its own current. We can't always set the pace to suit ourselves, much less the needs of others. Even our best friends can't always stop to lend a hand. If it's possible, some good Samaritan may notice our misfortune and swim over to offer us nourishment, encouragement, or another kind of help. These are very special people to whom God has given a unique gift—that of sensing our pain and loneliness and being able to swim to the side of the river and comfort us for a time.

> *It's important to remember that life proceeds at its own current. We can't always set the pace to suit ourselves, much less the needs of others. Even our best friends can't always stop to lend a hand.*

Those who listen to us, cry with us, hold us when we hurt, are God's gift. They may help us to clarify issues and gain a better perspective on our circumstances, or simply pray with us. Comfort lies in the fact that they are just there with us. We come to feel that we couldn't get through our plight without them. Even though they have given freely of their love, counsel, and care for us, at some point they too must return to the river—by God's will or their own volition. They know they must progress in their own journey, and so do we.

We have all been among those stuck on the side of the river at some time in our lives, in need of wise persons bearing gifts. Hopefully they have appeared and functioned well in giving of themselves, while we too have worked hard at resolving our issues and allowing God to heal our pain. If so, we may be ready to put a foot back into the river s-l-o-w-l-y, and begin the process of moving down its course once again. God will fulfill his promises in our lives and bestow greater and greater strength at each new bend in the stream.

CHAPTER 6

Stranded on the Side

How good it is to center down!
To sit quietly and see oneself pass
    by!
The streets of our minds seethe
    with endless traffic;
Our spirits resound with clashings,
    with noisy silences,
While something deep within
    hungers and thirsts
For the still moment and the
    resulting lull.

Howard Thurman

All of us can choose to stay immersed in the pain, entangled
in the garbage that pulled us to the side of the river in the first
place. One symptom of that choice is getting angry at others who
know that they can't stay there with us any longer. That anger
serves as a signal that we can't afford not to move on without
doing severe damage to our spirits. If you feel this kind of resentment building inside you, for heaven's sake, move on! You've got
to get back into the river to get out of the canyon!

As we move into the rapids of adulthood, we sense that we are rushing headlong down this river of life, being pushed by a whirlwind and constantly on the move. We may feel the stirrings of motion sickness, as if losing our perspective on life and our grasp of priorities. The neatly measured tempo of life often becomes a blur. Summer days that seemed to stretch on forever when we were children now pass in the blink of an eye. Events that occurred ten years ago seem to have happened just last week. There never seems to be enough time for everything, especially for reflecting on where we're going. We may even have a hard time fitting God into our lives. Life can be utterly exhausting!

Learning to pause in our journey helps us to see the world differently, but it's one of the most difficult things adults are called to do.

When we feel this way, we're approaching a point where we'll have to make some hard decisions. We know we can't go on like this forever. From time to time, we'll have to slow the pace of our lives. We may well need to feel dry land beneath our feet for a while. Learning to pause in our journey helps us to see the world differently, but it's one of the most difficult things adults are called to do. It seems impossible to take more time, when *time* seems to be the one thing that's running out. But doing so gives us a new perspective, a chance to recuperate, an opportunity to look at things in a healthier way.

Our need to pause by the side of the river is well understood. Since others have experienced that need before, some options may be mapped out already. For instance, most educational institutions provide sabbaticals for their faculty, literally a "sabbath time" for rest and replenishment. They know that teachers become weary after several years of giving themselves wholly to students, day in and day out. By taking time to be recharged both with recreation and new ideas, they can return to the river of education with fresh enthusiasm.

Like a career path, family life is also a long-term proposition. The choice to build a family is like driving a covered wagon down a well-traveled road. You have to pick your wheel tracks carefully because you may be in them a long time! Perhaps you've known a time when your family was in a very deep rut, unable to dislodge the wheels from your chosen track and head in a new direction.

Even your walk with God is not exempt from moments when you need time out.

Each member may be playing an expected role just to cope with life's exhausting routine, and it's beginning to get on everyone's nerves. As a group, you're all feeling tired. As individuals, you feel deprived of attention. What do you do? You get out the Rand-McNally Road Atlas and plan a much-needed family vacation—a tradition so time-honored in travel-conscious America that the film industry makes comedies about it, where every mishap is a cause for memories and laughter.

"Talking about it" needs to be balanced by "trying it out."... Relax occasionally during the problem-solving process. Some people call this allowing enough time to "incubate," allowing your thoughts to become behavior. We all need time to "digest" what we eat, before chewing some more.

—Don Koberg and Jim Bagnall,
The All New Universal Travel Guide

Even your walk with God is not exempt from moments when you need time out. Have you ever felt spiritually drained? You want to spend more time with God, but your prayer life doesn't seem to yield that strong sense of his presence the way it has in the past. You need a spiritual change of scenery. What do you do? If possible, you may spend a few days in silent reflection at a retreat center, seeking and discovering God in stillness that marks such a contrast from the busy-ness of everyday life.

LEARNING TO RECEIVE

Sometimes the warning signs of a needed time out are not as obvious, but they hit you just as hard. Perhaps you're fighting not to see them, which may mean that the lessons you're trying *not* to learn are very important. I speak from experience.

A few years ago I was packing late at night, getting ready to go on a ten-day speaking trip the next morning. A few hours earlier I'd felt a dull pain in my stomach, but "tough-it-out" me decided that one extra-strength Tylenol should fix me up. I thought that at the worst I might have the flu. Anyway, I only had a few more items to pack and I would be finished and ready to go.

Suddenly I felt as if a hot, sharp knife had ripped through my midsection! Gasping from excruciating pain, I collapsed next to the suitcase on my bed. In the mirror, I could see that I had turned as pale as sheetrock. My body first felt clammy, but within a few short minutes I felt like it was burning up. "What's happening to me?" I wondered, but I really didn't want to know. After all, I had places to go, people to see, speeches to make!

By morning I was almost delirious, barely able to dial my office for help. I managed to phone and ask for my assistant, Scott, to drive me to the doctor. I also asked someone to call and see if Gail Tucker was back from work yet, and if she could meet us at the doctor's office. Gail was my good friend, a nurse who worked four nights a week at a hospital. She also held down two other part-time jobs, so I didn't want to impose on her time. But I never went to hospitals and had rarely seen a doctor. I knew I would feel more comfortable if she were there. By this time my body was wrenched with pain and I knew something was very wrong.

Gail arrived at the doctor's office within minutes after Scott carried me in. The doctor didn't know exactly what was wrong either but I sensed his urgency. "I'm sending you right to the hospital and starting tests," he insisted. I heard my inner, bionic woman reply, "OK, I'll go, but I need to stop back by my place first and pick up a few things." Of course, I was too weak to even stand up!

"NO YOU WON'T," the doctor, Gail, and Scott yelled in unison. Gail froze my protest with a look of stern determination which she reserves for just such occasions. "I will go get the things you need, after we get you into the hospital," she said quietly but firmly. As Gail took the role of commander-in-chief, things begin to get done—and quickly. What a switch, to be at her mercy! I was so used to doing everything for myself, being the one in charge. Barely standing, I felt such relief letting my friend take over and being able to trust her expertise.

Gail met with the doctor before we left the office, and within minutes had me checked into the hospital. In short order she helped me undress and don that disgusting gown the hospitals provide. She adjusted my bed, met with the nurses, then drove over to my home where she packed my bags and delivered them to the hospital. When she returned, she unpacked my stuff, called my son, my office, my close friends, and sat beside my bed throughout the day. Then she drove to work that night without a minute of sleep!

As if you couldn't guess, I was beginning to feel more than a little guilty about Gail's sacrifice in taking care of me during this crisis. It was very hard for me to be on the receiving end of anything, much less such selfless service. As a little kid, I'd learned that I was going to have to take care of myself. Half of me encouraged her to go home and get some rest, while the other half of me was glad she wouldn't leave my side.

Three days later my condition had worsened. I was barely holding on. The doctors and nurses were frantic. Tests, X-rays, and more tests and they were still at a loss to diagnose what was wrong. Only semi-conscious and in great pain, I could sense I was sinking fast. My doctor informed me that the hospital's top surgeon was on his way and should arrive any minute. Their last resort was to have him open me up to see if he could find out what was the matter, but at this point I was too weak to care.

Just then the very confident-looking surgeon entered the lab, took one look at me curled up under the cold X-ray machine (for the third time that day), felt my weakened pulse, and with one simple pressure test, screamed at the medical staff something I can't quote exactly that sounded like, #!!#*#! "I know exactly what's wrong with her. Get her to surgery, *stat!*"—hospitalese for "right now, and don't stop for coffee."

I didn't have the flu, as everyone (including me) had supposed. My appendix had ruptured and with three days of no treatment, peritonitis had set in, along with the first signs of gangrene. After skillful emergency surgery, the next several days were touch-and-go, a kind of delirious blur as I fought to stay alive.

It took nine days to move past that crisis. When I had recovered sufficiently, a steady stream of friends came to visit me. My phone rang off the hook, lighting up the hospital switchboard from area codes across the United States. My room looked like I had just opened up a floral shop. With so much attention and activity whirling around me, it began to seem like old times. I was far from being out of the woods, however. I still had more to learn about how to let others do for me.

After my condition had stabilized, I was released from the hospital to spend the next month recuperating at home. My staff fixed up my living room like a master bedroom so I didn't have to walk upstairs. Friends brought in prepared meals, while Gail continued to sit by my bed, heat up the meals, drive me to the doctor for checkups, and even rent videos. To add insult to injury, I developed an infection in the incision so the wound wouldn't close. Gail took advantage of her training to change my bandages with expertise. Her care for me was incomparable, indispensable, and unforgettable.

"A crisis," writes Sue Monk Kidd, "is a holy summons to cross a threshold. It involves both a leaving behind and a stepping forward, a separation and an opportunity." In her wonderful book entitled *When the Heart Waits,* Kidd distinguishes between three kinds of crises we all have to face:

- One is the developmental transition, the kind of inevitable life stage that we explored in chapter three, wherein upsets are as unavoidable as when "a dog wanders through dominoes."

- A second type of crisis is an internal uprising, a sense of restlessness or disenchantment that signals a desire for change.
- Still another kind of crisis (and the kind we're discussing here) is the "intrusive event"—a death, illness, accident, or some other catastrophe that drops into our life unbidden. This crisis stuns us so that we cannot discover its meaning or the change it's brought about until some time has passed and our awareness has been given time to ripen.

Gradually, I learned two important lessons during my own period of crisis and recovery, that month of being temporarily moored by the side of the river: that slowing down is sometimes necessary; and that even compulsive givers need to learn how to receive. Those hard-earned lessons have helped me through many tough times.

The Book of Acts says that Jesus told his disciples, "It's more blessed to give than to receive." But for every giver there is a recipient. Jesus said that when you visit the sick, feed someone who is hungry, find clothes for a person who has none, it's as if you have done that kindness *to him.* I had always been the strong one, the giver. I didn't have much experience in receiving up to that point in my life. Gail's ministry to me taught me what it was like to be on the receiving end: I had been made to feel loved like a true child of God.

If you've known a time in your life when everything has come to a screeching halt, you know that it's also a time for decision. We either have to learn our lessons or run the risk of staying stuck.

Enforced bedrest also brought home to me the realization that coming to a full stop can be one of the best things that can ever happen to us. Like the shock from my burst appendix, it may take a mule kick just to get our attention! Being brought to a sudden stop can shake up our lives like never before. We may be forced to deal with life issues we haven't been willing to face. If you've known a time in your life when everything has come to a screeching halt, you know that it's also a time for decision. We either have to learn our lessons or run the risk of staying stuck.

> I recently found a simple but surprising sentence by St. Paul in 2 Corinthians 10:7, "You are looking only on the surface of things." Pain forces you to look below the surface. The tragedy is that so many of us never have the courage to choose to do that. Hence we waste much of our life in bitterness and complaint, always looking for something else, never realizing that perhaps God has already given us sufficient grace to discover all of what we are looking for in the midst of our own circumstances.
>
> —Tim Hansel, *Choosing Joy*

I learned invaluable lessons when my appendix brought my life to a halt. Being "set aside" for several weeks let me step out of the hectic world that I had created for myself. I began to appreciate the tremendous gift of time when the most I could do was nothing and the best I could do was heal. When I couldn't go to work, I could hear my staff saying, "About time!"

The truth is, I love both the ministry that I've been given and my work at the university. It's a wonderful atmosphere, and I have the support of a great staff. With never a dull moment, our office motto is, "We work hard, we play hard, and we laugh hard." Who would want to miss that?

Required time out on the side of the river can provide one of the most worthwhile experiences in life. Accepting that may be painful, but it brings tremendous growth for most of us. That pause that refreshes may uncover many lessons that we need to continue our journey.

OUR RELUCTANT RETREATS

None of us ever really wants to be out of the mainstream of life or stranded in still water. Even if we need time out there's never a "good time" for that to happen. Don't believe me? OK, pull out your calendar and tell me: what month or what year would you choose for a crisis to sideline you? If we knew when something was going to stop us in our tracks, we would catch the next train to Cucamonga and escape before the rails were closed!

My appendix couldn't have chosen a *worse* time to betray me. It was February and I was getting ready to go on the road for ten days to speak at some of the biggest events on my calendar. All canceled! The whole of February and March had been booked with traveling and speaking engagements. Canceled!

Two weeks after my hospital stay, my department at the university, the Institute for Outreach Ministries, was getting ready to take almost four thousand high school and college students on a one-week missions trip to Mexico. Nobody's one hundred percent effective at learning hard lessons. Against my surgeon's advice, I went along, but spent most of the day lying in a motor home, while Gail continued to change the dressing on my incision. Weakness and exhaustion taught me a valuable lesson: it didn't always have to be my show.

Have you ever been called for jury duty? Panic city. I have seen potential jurors bring card tables so they can work in the selection room. They sometimes form long lines at the phones and/or the fax machines to stay connected with their nine-to-five lives. Such behaviors may be symptomatic of a serious work addiction, but the simple fact of the matter is that we still have to function even when we're weathering a crisis that's put us on the sidelines.

Wouldn't it be wonderful if someone would create a remote yet secure place where we could all check in for weeks or even months—a riverside sanctuary of warmth and comfort where we could go when it was our time to be stranded, a retreat house where we could get away and deal with our issues? Don't we wish!

I envision not only a healing, Christian atmosphere where we could receive spiritual renewal and strong Christian counseling, but also a place of reunion. All the people we love would be moved to stop whatever they're doing and be there at the same time. This ideal rest stop would possess unlimited funds, so that our children would be taken care of, our own financial needs would all be met, and someone would even be hired to clean our houses, pay our bills, and do the grocery shopping in our absence. Isn't this what we all need? Your dream and mine says yes, but reality shakes its head slowly and says no. That dream can be so attractive that its unavailability becomes just the excuse to stop us from dealing with our issues and getting help. We must learn to deal with these crises in context, to learn and apply life's lessons whether we're pausing on the bank, swimming against the current, or cruising smoothly downstream.

THE PAINFUL EMBRACE

Pain is a built-in barometer that rises in pressure to indicate that something is deeply wrong inside, that some issue in our lives is crying out for attention.

One of the most powerful and obvious, yet most elusive lessons we can learn is that sometimes we just plain hurt. We are all human and none of us are exempt from pain. Pain is a built-in barometer that rises in pressure to indicate that something is deeply wrong inside, that some issue in our lives is crying out for attention.

Our natural tendency is to try to do everything we can to make the pain go away. We ask, "Why does *my* pain hurt so much?" We seek relief, some of us by drinking it away or by taking increased doses of medication. Others believe a new and exciting relationship, another warm and responsive body next to them in bed, will ease that pain. Still others try to bury their pain or even deny that it exists, only to find that it creeps up unexpectedly, often far worse than before, requiring a deeper reliance on avoidance and denial, rationalizations and excuses.

Our attempts to camouflage the pain are numerous and we often go to great lengths. Yet when we find the courage to embrace pain, we draw closer to its root issue and origin—the point at which real healing can begin. In imitation of Christ, we begin to know ourselves to be servants who suffer. Only then can

God begin to restore our health and heal our damaged and bruised spirit.

When we find the courage to embrace pain, we draw closer to its root issue and origin—the point at which real healing can begin.

THE CRISIS TOLL

Whatever is powerful enough in our lives to overcome the current and drive us to the river's edge can most certainly wear us out—physically, psychologically, emotionally, spiritually. We can feel like we've been run over with a Mack truck. It's not wise to move when we don't yet know what's broken!

Have you ever known a crisis so stressful that even after a good night's sleep you awoke exhausted, only to struggle through the day unable to make the simplest decisions and to perform everyday tasks that you've been doing for years? Has some burden in your life left you mute, without enough energy to say another word? Then you know the exhaustion that leaves you no choice but to rest at the side of the river.

Crisis can affect us deeply. It can slow down our productivity at work and shift our attitude so that we begin to hate our jobs. We may find that we can't give our families the attention they need, simply because we have nothing left to give. We may end up in the hospital because the stress from our pain is so great that it erodes our physical health. When we can no longer function, there's a great temptation to lie back and watch life go by.

We need to accept the fact that crises will take a toll, an inevitable consequence of tremendous stress. Pain is also a signal that we need to take better care of ourselves. Rest and exercise at the proper time are crucial. You rarely get both on the river: when the river's lazy, it makes no sense to paddle like mad, and when you're in white water, you can't lie back and watch the scenery!

Proper rest, a healthy diet, and regular exercise enable us to deal with crises in a healthier manner.

There is never a more difficult time on our journey than when we feel ourselves to be facing some problem or tragedy utterly alone.

A GIANT STEP

Solitude, the state of being alone and at home with ourselves, differs from *loneliness,* which entails feeling isolated, disconnected, hollow. The line between the two can be very fine. There is never a more difficult time on our journey than when we feel ourselves to be facing some problem or tragedy utterly alone. Loneliness can permeate every fiber of our being and reach to our very soul.

Sometimes a much more elemental pain may be the source of our loneliness, something which also pierces the innermost depths of our being. It is our *fear of abandonment,* the feeling that we will be left all alone.

Abandonment issues often spring from our early years, from having an absent father, a distant or unloving mother, or not receiving nurture when we needed it most. This fear influences our personality development at a very deep place. It may cause us to feel that those around us neither understand nor care about what we're going through. To us, they seem to be wrapped up in their own problems, oblivious to our pain. Since no one around us seems to be acting as a dam, we feel in danger of drowning.

Sometimes we feel this way because we haven't let other people know we hurt. Personality studies indicate that some of us are more private introverts and some of us are more gregarious extroverts. If you don't know what an introvert is thinking or feeling, it's because he or she hasn't told you. If you're in the dark about what an extrovert feels or thinks, it's because you haven't been listening.

Deep pain closes the gap by making introverts of us all. Many of us have learned to cover and mask our pain and issues very well.

We become such solid, silent Rocks of Gibraltar that no one will ever know if anything is wrong.

Some people are gregarious by default. They simply cannot bear to be alone, often because it triggers their fear of being abandoned and unloved. One of the biggest steps of growth for me was to learn how to be at ease with myself when no one else was around to help. At the core of this lesson was learning to love Carolyn Koons and not being afraid to be alone with her—to rest within her feelings, thoughts, and memories.

I took a giant step in self-awareness when a friend pointed out to me that I had not stayed home in the evening by myself once for an entire month! Nor was there one single weekend in which I hadn't booked a full slate of social activities—some informal, some official.

My pattern was clear. Every evening, I would stop at home just long enough to slip into something more casual and dash back out the door—to the office, to dinner, to a friend's, to a show, or whatever I could conjure up. On weekends when I wasn't speaking, I always had something fun planned to do. None of these activities was unhealthy in itself, and all were filled with the company of wonderful friends. But my *reason* wasn't healthy—I was afraid to be with just me. "Afraid" might seem too strong a word, but I'll use it because it made me face *myself.*

I made a decision to spend more time home by myself, without even the TV for company! I resolved to spend time with just me, to learn to enjoy those hours alone, and to use them wisely. This also meant not cluttering my evenings with work projects or other stuff to distract my mind. I thought, listened to music, worked in the yard or the garage. I drew, painted, read, rested, and prayed. And I was shocked to find that I loved it! Once I began simply to appreciate myself, God's unique creation, I knew more certainly that God loved me, even during those times that I did not love myself. Loneliness was no longer such a painful issue.

KEEPING OUR HEADS ABOVE WATER

Crises help us discover who our close, caring friends really are. When we hurt, we want those we trust to be with us, to support us, to help us understand what we're feeling, but most of all, simply to listen. It is at this time in our journey that our friends become like bright jewels in our lives. As Gail had done for me in my physical crisis, they may literally help us stay alive.

However, when we are truly stuck, we may put a lot of unrealistic expectations on our friends. We want to feel confident that at least one of our friends will always step in, to be by our side through the worst of times. If this doesn't happen, we may become deeply hurt and angered, and prone to feel they just don't care. After all, friends should check up on us! If they know we're in a crisis, they should call or write. These "shoulds" always compound the crisis.

We measure the depth of our friendships against our need, and often wonder why our friends don't measure up to this impossible standard. Certain reasons may keep them from being available in the ways we would like. Some want to put their heads in the sand and deny that anything is happening. Perhaps their own pain is so great that they feel they have nothing to give or wouldn't know what to say. It may be that they perceive our crises as something that we need to face alone. But when we hurt, we can't accept their refusal, much less their reasons, at face value.

We may find it hard to admit, but maybe our friends haven't reached out because they're afraid that whatever has befallen us may "rub off" on them. Or, maybe they simply don't know how much we're hurting. If we've gritted our teeth and tolerated the pain for a very long time, friends may think it's time for us to stop playing the Stoic, to seek healing, and to move on. When the pain becomes etched on our faces like a tracery of negative laugh-lines, they may be tempted to avert their eyes or avoid us altogether.

Friends may be likened to jewels, but only the rarest of jewels shines through no matter what the setting.

During my illness, I discovered how blessed I am to have good friends. But what if it was a divorce and not a burst appendix?

What if I were struggling with an addiction to alcohol or drugs or sex? What if my life was falling apart and I had to be admitted to a psychiatric hospital? Would my friends still send me flowers or visit? I have no way of knowing, though I'd like to think that they would.

Friends may be likened to jewels, but only the rarest of jewels shines through no matter what the setting. Special friends are like angels sent from God—one of his great blessings that we receive when we find ourselves alone by the side of the river, stranded, half-drowned with despair, in imminent danger of becoming stuck.

Think of the special people God has brought into your life at just the right moment. Some of these people are old friends, others relatives or new acquaintances, still others perfect strangers. Some may be sensitive professional counselors who can guide us through the roughest rapids along the way. Some are amateurs, but blessed with a very special gift meant just for us.

Your special friend may turn out to be a speaker at a conference or convention, a preacher at your neighborhood church, a friend at your bedside, or simply a companion at dinner. Whoever they may be, each one is chosen by God, someone special who senses your pain and reaches into the water to hold up your head.

Those special people in our lives are there to give that perfect piece of insight and understanding when we need it most. We hold their words close and take them into our souls, because they can help us to clarify the issues and get a better perspective. When someone prays with us and comforts us, it becomes clear that the timing could never be more perfect. This helping hand has come to us in God's good time, to bring us the encouragement and hope we need in order to move through our crises. Sometimes these special people remain in our lives as permanent friends. Often like a compassionate Lone Ranger, they move on. We will always remember them, thank God for them, recall their example, and hold ourselves ready to be used by God in that same way for someone else in need.

When we lie immobilized at the river's side, we turn inward for survival and have little to give. This is often when such people reach out and help us discover our need to receive—a need that some of us have kept carefully hidden or never knew was there. When I lay in the hospital at everyone's mercy, I was entirely dependent on the care of others for the first time in my life. I was amazed at my own reaction: I actually let them do it! This was a huge step for me.

Having friends be so totally giving was wonderful and hard all at the same time. I struggled to imagine how I could possibly repay them. Finally, I had to give up the whole idea of paying them back. I needed to simply appreciate and accept the fact that when I needed help, there were people there to give so freely and with so much love.

We all have a dream of what we want our lives to be, dreams filled with wonderful and happy visions. When our world is shaken, our dreams often become a casualty as we have to deal with a harsher reality. It's painful and disappointing to be stuck, but that is a choice we do not have to make. Our dreams need not vanish when we find ourselves by the wayside. The side of the river can also be a spot where we can rest, a place where we can learn and grow.

CHAPTER 7

Heeding the Warning Signs

Oh, what a tangled web we weave,
When first we practice to deceive!
Sir Walter Scott, *Marmion*

Resistance to suffering lies at the root of much of our resistance to change. We often say no to constructive change simply because we don't want to risk getting hurt and having to suffer the pain of withdrawal, rejection, or loneliness.

Overcoming that resistance responsibly is part of what Elaine Dickson has aptly called "cost control"—being sensitive to our limits but open to the challenge of positive change. Much of that change happens in the context of relationships, with God and others. As Jesus said, all of the commandments rest upon loving God and extending that love to our neighbors as much as to ourselves. Whenever we take the risk of letting go of what we may be holding onto for dear life, we learn more of what it means to love.

Yet at some time in our lives, most of us will disregard a warning sign and unwittingly invite unhealthy or destructive changes to intrude upon us and control our lives. Some warnings are simply restatements of the Ten Commandments: don't cheat, don't lie, don't steal. Some others warn about more specific dangers: don't try it; don't commit yourself before you count the cost; don't overspend, overeat, overindulge; don't speed; and above all THINK before you act.

Resistance to suffering lies at the root of much of our resistance to change.

What makes a desire become so all-encompassing that we are willing to suspend our values, our self-esteem, our sense of law and order to meet it? Perhaps that desire seems to meet a need, and giving it up seems paramount to renouncing the very thing we can't live without.

Like Adam and Eve who decided to take a bite from the fruit of the Tree of Knowledge, we convince ourselves to ignore the warning signs. We reason that God probably isn't looking, and that if he were, he would surely make an exception in our case. After all, warnings and rules were set up by others—like our parents, society, or the church. Now that we're grownups, we feel it's up to us to say yes or no.

Many of you might remember the first time you tried a cigarette. A friend of mine told me that he was offered one at the age of seventeen by an older companion to help him cope with his first "dear John" letter. The smoke tasted awful, but it lent him a certain romantic air and seemed to glamorize his melancholy. After that, whenever his self-esteem felt a little shaky, something inside suggested that a cigarette would ease his uncertainty and shore up his confidence.

What warning signs did he ignore? Messages about the potentially damaging effects of smoking were written on every pack, but to my friend they might just as well have been invisible. His desire to be more sophisticated soon gave way to simple dependence on nicotine, while inside he was convinced that smoking had made him a "man of the world."

Years later, as my friend struggled with emphysema, he would have paid everything he had ever spent on cigarettes for one clear breath. Yet he continued to smoke. He felt so badly about the disease that had claimed his vitality that a cigarette seemed the only cure for his depression.

Early in life, my friend chose a readily available crutch to compensate for the difficult work of building an independent self-image. His story is tragic and all too common. We can choose any number of ways to blind ourselves to mature responsibility to ourselves and to others. Whether the pain is real or imagined, we seek a temporary anesthetic for pain we seemingly cannot bear. We are convinced we need it and equally certain we can quit it anytime we desire—but tomorrow will always do.

DANGER AT THE EDGE

Many rivers contain a "weir," a danger point which is always clearly marked with a warning sign. For fishermen, however, the temptation to approach this spot often seems irresistible, just like all the other ingenious temptations to block out life's realities and responsibilities. Why? Because that is precisely where the "big ones" hide and reside.

Such a danger point is marked on the Kings River, just below Pine Flat Lake, a spot where the river looks especially angry, impatient, and anxious to get on its way. Water released from the lake boils over a dam and crashes into the riverbed, forming an artificial waterfall which experienced boaters treat with respect. The resulting current is so fast and dangerous that below the dam, a concrete wall spans the width of the river in an effort to slow the flow of the water.

As it approaches this barrier, the water appears smooth and calm, even though it is moving fast. That immense volume of water carries an enormous amount of energy, to which the obstruction of the concrete wall represents no more than a minor stumbling block. As the water trips over the barrier, an air space is created which in turn creates a violent backwash of water that churns like a giant washing machine turned on its side.

If anything—a log, a boat, a helpless human being—gets

trapped in this swirling mass of water, it can be forced to endure a vicious cycle. The weir drags its prey down, buffets it underwater, then shoots it skyward over and over. As if inexplicably tired of the game, the weir-water finally spits the object out much worse off for the ride.

The Kings River weir boasts a large steel cable which stretches a good two hundred feet or more along both banks and across the width of the river. Huge red signs hang from the cable bearing the warning, "DANGER, KEEP OUT!" The signs mean exactly that. Nevertheless, several years ago on the late news, I watched a report that still replays itself in my mind.

A woman standing on the shore happened to be experimenting with the zoom lens of her new video camera, taping her husband and his two friends as they fished. Ignoring the warning signs, they positioned their small boat just below the hungry weir. Fish are often plentiful near a weir, a safe haven with highly oxygenated water. Even as they fished, the underlying current silently dragged them closer, inch by inch.

The woman's husband casually waved at his wife, then cast his line directly into the mouth of the weir. As the tape captured the events in vivid detail, the back of the boat suddenly lifted straight up out of the water. Nose first, the boat and all three fishermen vanished into the mouth of the weir. It took two days to retrieve their battered bodies. Because of their desire for a big catch, these men had courted disaster and lost their lives.

What is it about temptation that makes us think, even for a moment, that we are exempt from the consequences of our actions? Newspapers, magazines, and television provide example after example of prominent people who disregard impossible odds in pursuit of money, power, sex, or public adulation.

In years past, such outrageous behavior was often covered up for the sake of avoiding scandal. During the last decade, however, we have learned how to talk about many taboos once considered family secrets—from sexual abuse to a variety of addictions such as alcohol, drugs, gambling, and sex. Because the public consequences for misconduct have become greater, the warning signs hung around these dangerous issues are that much bigger.

A celebrity athlete indulges his sexual fantasies with a numberless string of partners, and then discovers that he's contracted AIDS. Because his desire for fame outweighs the messages of his aging body, another athlete risks serious injury to keep playing just "one more year." A Wall Street entrepreneur abandons every principle of trading ethics to acquire an unimaginable fortune, and then smiles on his way to prison because he knows that much of his money awaits him upon his release. The reputation of a venerable statesman is drowned in the wave of a banking scandal. A teenage girl gets trapped in a web of violence in order to secure the affections of a man old enough to be her father.

What is it about temptations that makes us think, even for a moment, that we are exempt from the consequences of our actions?

We are shocked and dismayed, but sympathetic, because we see in many such stories a magnified image of ourselves. Over the course of our lives, each of us acquires a variety of attractive attachments. Their lure bears a strong resemblance to the siren call of the weir. The warning signs are posted everywhere, but we foolishly ignore them.

Anyone who thinks that their portion of the river is free of weirs had better look again. Make a list of the substances or activities that are habitually part and parcel of your life, perhaps coffee, cigarettes, chocolate, or TV soaps. Include the behaviors you believe define your personality, such as being helpful, cheerful, assertive, or brutally honest, no matter what it costs or who it might hurt. Also list whatever you *avoid* at all costs, which may include things like x-rated movies, cocaine, paying your taxes late, or swimming in water over five feet deep.

Your list may not be spectacular or scandalous enough to get your picture into *People* magazine, but we all have the potential to become entrapped when we least expect it. We glide over the smooth, ominous water until we are sucked under by the undercurrent and trapped in the backwash of a life-destroying cycle. Sooner or later, just as if we were in a weir, we discover that our fatal attraction has played us falsely, ultimately taking everything from us and offering nothing in return. It will pull us under and spit us out time and again, until our lives are totally consumed and out of our control. Progress stops, life loses its joy, and we are stuck.

We adults often rationalize away our own responsibility when misfortune strikes. We claim to have been at the wrong place at the wrong time. After all, we reason, the warning signs certainly didn't apply to us, people who were clearly in control of our behavior and choices. We explain or blame, hoping to emerge with our honor or our relationships intact.

We need to see that the self-centered "adult" who concocts these rationalizations is no adult at all, but an addictive personality that comes out of hiding for a moment to make a convincing case for a foolish obsession. When a person has never really learned to take responsibility for his or her own actions, the consequences are virtually always a tragic surprise.

The weir and the river—along with mood-altering chemicals and sexually transmitted diseases—operate according to the amoral principles of physics or biology. It is not the weir's fault that the fishermen drowned. They drowned because their inordinate desire to catch fish overcame their good judgment. In the river as in life, ignoring warning signs is reckless, and in many cases, deadly. Emotional obsessions, too, generate a predictable range of feelings that have little to do with goodness or evil.

Heeding warnings often demands sacrifice, which is never easy. "Every sacrifice," writes Christopher Fremantle, "involves suffering. . . . If the suffering is not voluntarily accepted, it turns into bitterness, as surely as Lot's wife turned into salt." No one submits to suffering without a struggle, but the kind of suffering that springs from sacrifice yields a new and better life.

BEWARE OF SMOOTH APPEARANCES

Do you remember Rumpelstiltskin, the little man who promised to free the young queen who spun straw into gold for him, if she could only guess his name? In a wonderful poem by Glyn Maxwell, Rumpelstiltskin is so enraged when the queen succeeds that he lies and tells her that his name is Zed, to which the queen replies that his anger is turning him red. The poem ends this way:

"Liar!" he cried. "I'm turning blue."
And this was absolutely true.
And then he tore himself in two,
As liars tend to have to do.

In the poem, Rumpelstiltskin alone suffered from his deceit. More often, when we willingly deceive ourselves and others, we aren't the only ones who get hurt. Others may believe us, buy our safe-looking line, cross it, and then pow! Everyone is slapped with a white-water reality which looks and feels very different from the smooth façade they had trusted.

There is another river hazard called an *eddy*, much less obvious than the well-marked weir, but which offers a perfect illustration of the destructive power of deception. I discovered the effects of an eddy when I took a trip with one of my students down the Kings River in a canoe. Having run the river several times in rubber rafts, we decided to see how far we could get in a more fragile craft. Canoes are quite buoyant but difficult to maneuver in rough water. We wanted to see how many sections of white water we could get through without getting flipped.

The student I recruited for this fool's errand was named Glenn. Electing to take the run without someone to bail water, the two of us pushed off from shore. We entered a safe distance from the weir but had only seconds to straighten the canoe's course downriver before we hit white water. In a raft it didn't matter so much if we hit the rapids sideways or even backwards. With the canoe, however, it was an entirely different story.

We both yelled (I *screamed*) through the first set of rapids as the canoe responded with quick, crisp movements to every ripple, wave, and hole. We made it through and emerged only slightly wet. As we prepared for the next stretch of rough water, I saw a cluster of rocks that formed a tiny island in the middle of the river. We decided to stay on the right side, where the river seemed to flow more smoothly. It seemed a good choice.

As the river widened and calmed, I watched as the two currents which had separated above the rock island began to merge. It was a beautiful sight, but I had a strange feeling when I observed something in the river I had never seen before. It looked as though someone had drawn a perfectly straight line across the entire width of the river. Along that line was a five-inch fold created as these two currents came together. We had to cross it. I didn't know anything about negotiating this fold in the river. As if we had all the time in the world, we debated about what to do. Should we bisect the little fold of water, or maybe turn the canoe sideways and ease it over the line?

As it turned out, we didn't have long to think about it. As we approached the line, the canoe capsized without warning. Glenn and I were thrown quite a distance downstream from that treacherous five-inch fold. We swam to the side of the river, where we sat and watched as the inverted canoe shot to the surface time and again like a breaching whale, only to sink back down into that fold of water that held it fixed in the current by an invisible force, tight as a tractor beam from Star Trek. I shuddered to think that we might have been underneath it!

That strange five-inch fold in the river hadn't looked like anything compared to the rapids. We later learned that our trouble on the river was due to what's called an eddy. On the surface the water appears glassy and smooth, except where the innocent-looking line forms. Below the surface, however, the two merging currents go to war. We had been easily deceived by the river's easy-going appearance. We were having fun, unaware of what was below the surface until it hit us. How could something that had looked so innocent have been so destructive?

The problem with the eddy is precisely that it is so deceptive. When you're traveling in a canoe or kayak, it can be the most frightening part of the river. Water that looks like silky glass on the surface can suck you under in an instant into an overpowering undercurrent. The dangers of a weir are visible, with tons of thunderous water churning ferociously on the surface. The eddy's potential for destruction is deceptive, lying hidden, yet ready to paralyze and devour its victims.

> *Many things in life can look*
> *perfectly safe on the surface.*

Deception smacks us in the face every day of our lives. Deception is the voice of the serpent in the garden of Eden saying, "Go ahead, eat the forbidden fruit. You will not die." It's the character of Sportin' Life in the opera *Porgy and Bess*, singing at a picnic to a gullible crowd, "The things that you're liable to read in the Bible, it ain't necessarily so." It's you and I when we say to ourselves, "Oh, this is an innocent relationship. We won't get really involved." Or, "A little of this or that won't hurt me. I can try a taste and give it up. Anyway, if I take just a little, no one will ever know."

Many things in life can look perfectly safe on the surface, but nothing takes your breath away more quickly than discovering their hidden danger. You feel betrayed, and the most painful forms of betrayal are the ones we visit on ourselves. When we live a lie, we hold the world at arm's length, afraid to let anyone see inside. Then, as M. Scott Peck has observed in his book *People of the Lie*, we become so ingrained in the habit of telling an untruth that an ever greater part of ourselves becomes one with the lie. Living a lie splits our personality, like the split current that produces the deceptive turbulence of an eddy. One part is the polished image we present to the public; the other part is the damaged self whose wounds we nurse in private.

What are some of the little ways you fool others, or even yourself? "Denial," as comedian Al Franken quips, "ain't just a river in Egypt!" What are the things about your life that you would just as soon others wouldn't see? Living honestly from the inside out is a life-long process, never perfectible but certainly in need of continuing improvement. That's what life on an ever-changing river is all about.

If you're stuck in a destructive habit, a deceitful lifestyle, or a dishonest relationship, stop everything. Most of all, stop pretending that everything is OK. Everything is *not* OK. If you're being tumbled over and over in an eddy, you're not going anywhere until you deal with the source of the problem: *yourself*. And you may eventually sink below the surface for good. Get out of the river and get well, with the help of a professional if necessary. Take the risk to admit that you aren't what you say you are, which is the only way to get on with your life.

It's difficult to feel one way and to act another. Those two opposing currents are sure to churn you up inside. For example, if you feel unhappy at your core, there is little you can do to minimize that pain. Keeping up the pretense of contentment becomes increasingly difficult when you consistently feel like a failure inside. The gap between your inner and outer realities grows enormous, and soon you find yourself on a downward spiral, your rapid descent greased by disappointment and anger.

One of the most powerfully deceptive eddies in life is the disturbance of an extramarital relationship. Carrying on an affair means your boat is floating in the water of a lie. The relationship may seem justifiable, like the smooth water on the surface of the eddy. Whatever the rationale, the lie is that such a relationship is OK.

If you are or have been caught in the eddy of adultery, take a look beneath the surface. An underlying need may hold the reason for an illicit relationship, and it's seldom what you think. Perhaps you believe that clandestine romance is the drug you need to fill a void in your life. You may never have been willing to face the problems in your marriage or else a fundamental problem in yourself. You may expect that a spicy love affair will compensate for what you haven't found the courage to heal.

Whenever you choose the intense feelings of *being in love* over the hard work of *loving someone* in a committed relationship, the objects of your affection are not seen for who they really are, only for what they seem to provide. And if you're involved with someone at another's expense, you're in treacherous waters that can close over you suddenly and unexpectedly. Don't be fooled by one eddy of infidelity after another until you ruin your life.

WATCH YOUR STEP

How vulnerable we become when we live a lie! Some of you may shake your head as you read this and exclaim, "Boy, I'm glad I'm honest. I'm faithful in my marriage, not on drugs, happy with my life. I don't even smoke! Too bad the rest of the world is so messed up."

Remember what Jesus said to the crowd who were bent on executing the woman accused of adultery: "If any one of you is without sin, let him be the first to throw a stone at her" (Jn 8:7). "All have sinned and fall short of the glory of God," writes St. Paul. The fact is that certain weirs and eddies swirl across the route of every one of us over the course our lives. No one lives completely within the light of truth, although that's where we'd all like to be.

Since I first gave my life to Christ, I have become aware of how easy it is to construct an ideal Christian image. Sugar, spice, snips, snails, and puppy dog's tails have been suggested as building materials for little boys and girls. Christians face a fascinating temptation to fashion a kind of angelic personality by stitching together all of the Christian virtues: faithfulness, honesty, patience, kindness, long-suffering, joy—you know, little things like that. It's pure imagination, of course, but when we fail to measure up to such an ideal, we tend to feel tremendously guilty. To ease that feeling, we often pretend that we're something we're not—namely, perfect.

A version of this mindgame sometimes happens to me when I'm on a speaking engagement. Whether I'm conducting a seminar or speaking to a large convention, the people sense my excitement, feel my energy, and sometimes they want more. The trouble is that even I run out of energy from time to time. My tank may be bone dry after I've given a talk before a large group.

Even so, I get satisfaction at times by leading people to believe that my energy is boundless, that my ability to be fully present to someone else never leaves me. It's some variant of the Messiah complex, I suppose—Carolyn Koons' attempt to be the one who saves the world. When I'm motivated by that false image, I'll try to pretend that I'm not tired... all to no avail. I can't imagine how many unsuspecting people have been disappointed in what I've been able to give simply because I couldn't admit I was exhausted.

If we can do all things through Christ who gives us the strength, can we ask the Lord for the strength to admit our weaknesses? We are all human, finite creatures who find ourselves out of control on the river, always farther from the truth than we'd like. Those of us who know this are humbly grateful for every second chance at life, and ever watchful lest that same insidious untruth that has capsized us in the past should sneak up on us again.

COURAGE TO CONTINUE

Have you ever wondered why life's journey seems so easy for some people? First of all, it's not true. The journey is hard for everyone; it's just hard in different places. Where are your hard places, the spots where you suddenly feel "up the creek without a paddle?" Those are the places where you may come to feel that you have no choice, that you are truly stuck.

This may be the most difficult time to decide to change: when some part of you is convinced that you have no choice at all. To my everlasting good fortune, I have come to know those who have gotten back in the river when it appeared that the only choice was to give up. These courageous people have learned to swim and stay afloat in an altogether different way, when they could well have chosen to let the waters close over them.

This may be the most difficult time to decide to change: when some part of you is convinced that you have no choice at all.

Many of you may have read the inspiring story of Joni Eareckson Tada, a woman who, though paralyzed from the neck down, found a way to continue to share her creativity, talent, and faith with thousands of people. Many others like her have matched great disappointment with great courage. One is my dear friend

Sonja, who was stricken with cancer at the young age of twenty-four.

Sonja suffered through several surgeries and aggressive chemotherapy. Among other painful rituals, she was forced to have her blood drawn every week for eighteen months. Through it all my friend remained as eager for life as anyone I've ever known. If she felt really awful, Sonja would plan a party. Sometimes she would sleep through it, but the point was to stay in joyful contact with loving friends.

Sonja's days were always too short. No number of shopping trips, good books and movies, ice cream parlors, late-night escapades, or new flavors of coffee seemed to satisfy her irrepressible spirit. She hadn't expected cancer to be discovered one sunny morning, but she managed to live with its reality—as if her own heart had set up a rhythmic whisper for her soul to hear: "Live, live, live."

I don't think Sonja ever got used to having a needle stuck in her veins. Privately, she allowed her tears to flow, and she asked others to help her laugh. I remember the time she led me out of the hospital and called over her shoulder, "C'mon, we're out of here! I'm hungry!" But my friend wasn't just looking for something to eat; she was hungry for a full life in spite of the challenges presented by her cancer. This is what her indomitable spirit achieved.

Sonja's cancer is now in remission, but even in her illness she never lost sight of her need for the love of friends and family to be the touchstones for her life, rather than let her disease fulfill that function. Women like Joni and Sonja show us that courage is an elixir for life, the way to overcome a fatalistic entrapment in hopelessness. They help us to discover how to enrich life with meaning and purpose, even when meaning itself seems to be lost. This is the kind of river lore that has helped to keep me out there paddling.

LEAN INTO THE ROCK

One final hazard I learned from my rafting adventures: if you see a big rock in the river, it's best to steer right for it. All the rafting guidebooks will tell you the same thing: when the water's just flippin', "lean into the rock." That's good advice, but your first instinct is to panic and steer the raft away from ominous, immovable obstructions like river boulders.

If you can overcome your fear and lean into the rock, the water rushes up against the rock and creates a fluid surface that lets you slide over the obstacle and shoot downriver. The current will carry you smoothly over or around it. Take it from me, the guidebooks are right; it works every time! The way to conquer river potholes is to steer straight down the middle, lean into the rock, and chug, baby, chug! Don't backpaddle or lose your courage and make for the side, but let the rock add to your energy as you make your way down and through.

God wants people who are willing to chug through that water, all the while leaning on him.

I find this to be an effective formula for white-water rafting and a recipe for life as well. God wants people who are willing to chug through that water, all the while leaning on him. We will no doubt encounter some fiendish potholes and manage to get thoroughly soaked, but that's OK. Getting wet is part of the cost of winning.

Many times in our lives we may feel like we're sinking. The waters of change and crisis seem to be closing over us for the last time. My first few years with Tony was just such a time. As we worked through one traumatic episode after another in our effort to build a loving relationship, I often felt myself drowning. However discouraged I became, I kept praying: "There is an end to this rough water. I know we'll get through it. Loving God, just take me one step at a time." I know from experience that there is clear water at the end of every stretch of rapids. If we can avail ourselves of the grace to reach it, God will show us the way.

Lean into the rock. That's exactly what God says to us, "Lean on me." Don't go through the river of life as though you're piloting a sailboat in a gentle breeze. Read the river and take what you learn into your heart. Lean into the Rock of our salvation, who is

God in Jesus Christ. That's how you'll avoid becoming stuck and enabled to come through the raging water.

Lee Webber, a poet who lives in Santa Rosa, California, just a few miles from the beautiful Russian River, wrote a poem entitled "Crossings" which speaks about that fundamental revelation:

> I came to the swift, raging river,
> And the roar held the echo of fear;
> "Oh Lord, give me wings to fly over,
> If You are, as You promised, quite near."

> But He said, "Trust the grace I am giving,
> All-pervasive, sufficient for you.
> Take My hand—we will face this together;
> But My plan is, not over, but through."

PART THREE

Moving On

Now that we have considered the specific aspects we may encounter in our journey through life, I would like to share more of my own story with you. More than anything else, what has moved me to write this book is the personal knowledge that God stands ready to bring healing and transformation into our lives. I believe it is never too late, that we are never too far gone to get unstuck and move on to an ever more wonderful life, richly filled with God's blessing.

I know this because it happened to me. Like Tony, I had come into the world unwanted, despised by my parents, and consequently desperate for affection. Every time I'm hugged as an adult, it seems to make up for every embrace I was denied as a child. In my childhood and teen years, I acted out defiantly, as if to display the scars of my own upbringing.

Then God entered my life through the gentle, unfailing love of Christian people. Their love enabled me gradually to face my pain and seek healing for it, a process which still goes on to this day. After publishing the story of my early experiences with Tony, I wrote a second book about my own painful and difficult journey, which I entitled *Beyond Betrayal*.

In this last section, I will share three episodes from my life. Through these particular events, loving friends helped me finally to make peace with my past and to move freely and with confidence toward the future. I want to talk frankly about barriers and guides along life's river, and how all of us can be better led in life's adventure. In sharing my own painful experience of growth and change, I want to draw a connection between the creative process and the pursuit of possibility, and to offer some simple principles for getting unstuck. After that, it's time to stop reading and get going, a decision that's entirely up to you and me!

CHAPTER 8

Being *"Born Again"* Is Just the First Step, Not the Last

Lord, keep me from making daily
payments to the past and from pre-
paying some future fantasy. Help
me know I am debt-free today to
spend my gifts of choice saying yes
to life... or sometimes no if no is a
better way.   **Billie Pate**

T he realization that I could get
unstuck from the pain that
kept me pinned to the riverbank took a long time to gel in my
mind. At the very beginning of that process, I thought that I was
the only one that carried the burden of deeply painful memories.
Mine stemmed from a hellish childhood, but after years of
wrestling with the pain of my past, I began to realize that we all
bear such burdens.

While our pain stems from different sources and rises up in our
lives at different points, the impact can be devastating. It still
astounds me how I completely despaired of being released from
my own burdens. As our rafts struggle against the dead weight of

the past, our journeys down life's river are often laborious and sluggish. We cultivate the art of concealing those things that we don't want anyone else to know—the secrets, the pain, all that we're afraid to look at and deal with.

I was a master of that subtle art. Although I appeared to be enthusiastic, always willing to work the room and make connections, I kept the dead weight from my past neatly tucked away. I dragged it with me wherever I went, until God showed me a way to seek and find real healing. This is the story of how that gift was given.

A SIGN OF HOPE: THE TRACKS OF MY TEARS

I was just sixteen years old, a junior in high school, but as far as I was concerned, my life was over. I was distant and desperately lonely, my anger as hard and piercing as a hot rivet. I had been drinking heavily at parties since I was in the sixth grade. I would frequently get so drunk that I couldn't even remember what guy I had made out with the night before, and usually didn't even know his name. Several times I had narrowly missed being arrested by the police for vandalism as my friends and I sped down alleys with our car lights off to escape capture.

Another form of entertainment my friends and I enjoyed was to break into people's cabins and trash the insides. We took whatever we wanted to use as target practice, then set up our treasures in front of a hill, took aim with our hunting rifles, and proceeded to blow them apart. The local newspaper offered a reward for information leading to our arrest. The police were never close to discovering us, but even if they had been, I really wouldn't have cared.

At only sixteen I felt much older and very tired. Those who knew me warned that I would end up in jail the way I was going. My own attitude was rather fatalistic: sooner or later I would probably get caught. It was just a matter of time. Most of all, I felt nobody cared if I lived or died, until a telephone call from someone I didn't know changed my life.

"Hello, Carolyn. You don't know me, but I've heard a lot about you. My name is Jean Fonner," said the pleasant voice on the other end of the line. I wondered why she had called. I soon found out. After a few sentences of small talk she continued, "Carolyn, one of the reasons I'm calling is that I would like to invite you to our church, Bethany Baptist Church in Long Beach. We have a wonderful youth group here. In fact, I think you know several of the kids that attend. They go to your high school."

When Jean mentioned their names, I couldn't believe it. These were the last kids in the world I wanted to hang around with! They were those "Christian kids," as we called them. Some of them actually carried their Bibles with them to school. A couple of times a week they would sit on the lawn during lunch break and have what they called Bible studies. A gang of us would do anything to disrupt their meetings. We used to barge into the middle of their study circle, accidentally on purpose. We'd drop our Cokes on them, throw food at them, and kick the Bibles out of their hands. Sometimes we just stood around them and yelled cuss words.

I didn't like Christians. I'd actually tried to burn down a church once. Churches were always a convenient target for my contempt. I mean that literally. When a group of "holy rollers" built a small church with a tin roof just down from our house, my friends and I harrassed them. When they were holding evening services—which seemed like about every night of the week—we would get our shot guns and drive by and shoot at the church. The thunder of the shot pellets ricocheting off the tin roof could be heard for blocks. After a while the side of the church displayed hard evidence of our target practice.

I especially didn't want anything to do with the Christian kids at my high school. This woman was definitely barking up the wrong tree. With several terse cuss words, I abruptly told Jean that I wasn't interested in going to church and that I didn't like Christians anyway. She seemed to ignore my rejection and went on to make a very startling and direct statement.

"Carolyn, I think you will find some answers to your life at our church."

Was I mad! Didn't this woman listen? Who did this Jean Fonner think she was? She didn't know anything about me. I wanted nothing to do with the church or with Christians, and especially with this God they always talked about. I couldn't trust the people I could see; how was I supposed to trust a God I couldn't see? I was livid as I continued to cuss Jean out. I slammed the phone down, but her last words echoed in my ear. "Carolyn," she said quietly, "I'm going to pray for you."

Jean was not only prayerful, she was persistent. She kept calling me, as if I had never rejected her, and kept inviting me to the youth group. She even visited my family's little eight-by-forty-foot trailer. She simply wouldn't give up. God must have known that I really needed someone who was tough, someone who would hang in there with me and take my guff. He put this lady in my life who was not going to give up on Carolyn.

The scariest thing I ever did was when I finally attended that church for the first time. I walked into the youth group, and to my complete surprise never saw a more exciting place in my life. The energy in the room was electrifying. I spent an incredible hour there, but it terrified me. I left quickly, without saying goodbye.

One of God's miracles was that these Christian people continued to be patient with me. After several months of going to church, running out of the building, claiming I would never go back, I finally made the most important decision of my life. I knew that I couldn't live as I had any longer. I wanted my life to be different—in what ways I just didn't know. It seemed to my sixteen-year-old mind that I had two choices: God or jail. Quite honestly, I didn't know which choice scared me more. I just hated the way my life was going. I decided to ask God to come into my life, to work a miracle in me. And praised be his name, he did.

I prayed a simple prayer that day: "God I want you in my life. I don't really know what all of this means. I just know I don't want to live like this anymore. I want my life to be different. Please, God, come into my life."

In an instant the strangest thing happened. Tears began to flow from my eyes and run gently down my cheeks. It wasn't out-of-control sobbing. I was quietly sitting with my head bowed while tears streamed down my face. I captured some of the tears on the end of my finger and stared at my damp hand, not quite believing it. I was sure I hadn't cried in years. At least, I couldn't remember it.

I did remember the hurt of being desperately lonely through most of my life. I recalled vivid scenes of growing up in a very abusive and violent alcoholic home. I remembered being so miserable and feeling so rejected that I desperately wanted to cry, but couldn't. One time I was in so much emotional pain that when the tears didn't flow, I started pinching the tear ducts under my eyes to see if I could squeeze out one measly tear. Still nothing came. I was so despondent that I raised my fists and started smashing them against my eyes. Anything just to weep, yet my stubborn eyes stayed dry. It was as if any expression of tenderness had been ripped out of my body, leaving a hard, unfeeling shell.

Offering myself to God that day was the most frightening thing I had ever done. I had learned at a very early age that you can't trust anyone. If I was going to make it in this life, I was going to have to make it on my own. I couldn't count on anyone to reach out and help me in any way. I didn't trust people to keep their word. I risked more at that moment than at any time in my life. I risked letting go and taking a very big step into the unknown. I had asked for God, whom I couldn't even see, to come into my life. Me, of all people! I was going to trust this invisible God!

I did it because I had given up all other hope. I said to myself, "I will either take this scary step and ask God to come into my life, or I'll end up in prison." I chose God, chose life, and, in that instant, a miracle occurred. God showed me something. It might not sound like much to you, but God showed me my tears. These freely flowing droplets of salty water were a tremendous sign, not only that God was in me, but that he would restore to me all of the emotions that had been sucked out of my life. By the tracks of my tears, God revealed his promise that he would heal me.

A NEW BEGINNING

Becoming a Christian in such a dramatic way was really a remarkable experience. I felt as if God had suddenly picked me up and turned me around one hundred and eighty degrees, then set me down again to move in a totally different direction. A whole new world began to open up for me. After all those painful years, Carolyn Koons finally had a real reason to live. It was a new beginning, and I was eager to drink in every moment.

What was equally amazing was that I honestly felt different. Something inside me had changed. For the first time, I was genuinely happy, excited about every day and each moment in it. Before I found God, anger had seeped out of every fiber of my being. I hated everybody, especially my abusive parents, whose anger was more than a match for mine. I had lived such a destructive life—sort of like King Midas in reverse, seemingly hurting or damaging everything I touched.

God began to change all of that—not instantly but gently, gradually, with a quality much like Jean Fonner's invitation to join her church. At first my external circumstances didn't change a lot, but so much was going on inside me that even I could tell the difference.

For the first time I wore a smile on my face. Not only was I excited about today, I even looked forward to tomorrow. I discovered what a joy it was to be part of a loving, Christian family, which the members of that church had become for me. At last, after sixteen years, Carolyn Koons had a reason to live and to laugh!

My life was changed so radically that I couldn't get enough of God and this new life. Every time the doors of the church opened, I was the first one through them. I loved the songs we sang and all of the music in our church. Believe me, ours was a singing church! I clung to those choruses and the music sent healing to my soul. I wouldn't miss a single service of worship.

Not knowing the difference between Genesis and Revelation and barely able to read anyway, I struggled to tap the wisdom of the Scriptures. The messages from our pastor, Dr. Bob Hubbard, always seemed to be exactly what I needed. I would always sit close to the front of the congregation so that I wouldn't miss a single word.

The church and especially its high school youth group became my new life and my new family. It was alive, but far more important, for the first time *I* was alive. My new life was soon filled to overflowing with youth activities, church services, Bible studies, memorization of Scripture, skid row mission services, outreach trips to Mexico, beach jaunts, retreats, choir rehearsals, youth rallies. This was a whirlwind totally different than the black tornado my life had been before I became a Christian. And I loved every minute of it. As I grew in faith, I loved the Lord more every day.

Despite my newfound joy and growth, there were aspects about theology that I didn't understand. After all, I hadn't been raised as a Christian. One message I struggled with was this: if you have a problem, just "give your burdens to the Lord." Even though I understood what that meant and believed it, I couldn't seem to make this principle work in my life. *How do you really do that? I wondered. How do you give your burdens to the Lord?*

I listened to other ways of putting this same message. "When your burdens get too heavy, and your problems get too big," church leaders would say, "just leave it at the cross." Or, "Leave it at the feet of Jesus. He will take all of your cares away." When I heard that preached or when we sang about it, I had no trouble believing it. Many times, I remember coming forward in the church service and kneeling at the altar. And I clearly sensed that God heard my every word.

Prayer had become a big part of my life. Whenever I prayed, I would feel good for a while, but the feeling wouldn't last. You see, even though God had reached down to save me and truly turn my life around, even though I was growing in the Lord and loved my new life, buried deep in the innermost core of Carolyn Koons were cutting wounds from a truly desolate childhood. The pain from these wounds was so strong and so ingrained, that I still wasn't sure that this wonderful God in whom I now believed so strongly, could heal their hurt.

Even though my pain gnawed at me every day, I didn't know how to describe it. I was also afraid to get in touch with my pain, so I couldn't talk about it even if I wanted to. Anyway, I had never heard anyone in our church of over fifteen hundred members talk about these hidden feelings. When I looked around the congregation, everyone seemed so "victorious." They all seemed to walk around with confident smiles on their faces—much like mine! In fact, our church's theme song was "Victory in Jesus, Our Savior Forever."

Dutifully, joyfully, victoriously, I prayed and I sang and I tried to leave my heavy burden of pain at the cross... but it didn't always work. I didn't know if the pain would ever go away. No one seemed to know that for me prayer didn't always open the door to immediate victory.

Even though I projected the image of a brand new Christian who was ecstatic about this new life, our youth pastor, Louie, could sense something was wrong. I think he could see it when he looked at my face, as if my anguish had become deeply etched in a way that I couldn't hide from perceptive eyes. "What's the problem, Carolyn?" he would say, "What's bothering you?"

I hesitated, in part because I still found it difficult to be vulnerable. I wasn't sure if I wanted to broach this subject. I didn't want anyone to think that I wasn't victorious! Then again, Louie was my friend. He and his family had meant a lot to me, and he'd always shown a special interest in my journey of faith. I decided to take the risk.

Gingerly, the way you'd run your tongue around a troublesome tooth, I opened up the topic. "Louie, I know I'm a Christian," I began. "And I know God has changed my life. But what about all those things I *did* before I became a Christian? Don't I need to go back and deal with some of that stuff, ask God's forgiveness? Should I have a talk with the police or apologize to the people I hurt?"

I paused and took a deep breath. Louie sensed that I wasn't finished and waited patiently. Then I popped the question that lay at the root of my innermost pain. "Louie, what about all of the things that *happened* to me before I became a Christian? How do I deal with those?" That was as far as I could go with my confidant, who was sensitive enough not to pry.

Louie said all the right things in response. He gave me an orthodox Christian reply, with no way of knowing that I needed much more than a religiously correct answer. "No, Carolyn, you don't have to go back and try to change the things of the past. And in most circumstances, you don't have to go back and apologize to everyone. You see, Carolyn, your past has been forgiven. Christ died on the cross for your sins. He paid the price for you and now you are set free. You have been cleansed by the blood of Jesus."

Louie continued, "It's just as Scripture says—you are 'born again.' 'Old things are passed away and all things are become new.' It is as if you now have two birthdays. One is your natural birthday and the other is the day that you became a Christian. Carolyn, you've been given a new start, a new chance in life. You can act as if the day you were truly born was the day that you asked Christ into your life. You never have to worry about your past again."

He's right, I thought. *This is the answer I needed to hear. I am born again. I am a new creation in Christ. My life really is different.* So I did what I think a lot of Christians have done, and still do. I reached into my mental toolbox, took out a heavy-duty saw, and carefully sliced away all of that dead wood from the tree of my heart, hoping that old things would truly pass away and I would never have to deal with them again.

All the cuttings of my pain, present and past, lay on the floor of my heart. Taken one by one, they didn't seem like much of a burden. Collectively they were actually very heavy, with sharp ends that could still wound me. I bound the cuttings with the twine of my own hope. Then I found I could breathe a little more easily and sing more openly of "Victory in Jesus," along with all the other Christians I thought I knew.

Yet every once in a while after that conversation with Louie, Pastor Bob would start talking as if he knew that those painful branches still cut my heart. At first I would sit there in the pew, fearful that my pain would show. Then I would remember the promises of Scripture: "You are born again... old things are passed away." Then I would relax only a little, disturbed by a feeling that there were a lot of Christians just like me, binding and burying their pain.

No one talked about it, so neither did I. I became so skilled at tightening the cords that if I heard a message that came close to what I held so close to my heart, I would think to myself, *This is a great sermon. I'm sure it's going to minister to a lot of other people today.*

Modern Christianity, in dramatic reversal of its biblical form, promises to relieve the pain of living in a fallen world. The message, whether it's from fundamentalists requiring us to live by a favored set of rules or from charismatics urging a deeper surrender to the Spirit's power, is too often the same: The promise of bliss is for NOW! It simply isn't necessary to wrestle with internal struggle and disorder. Just trust, surrender, persevere, obey. The effect of such teaching is to blunt the painful reality of what it's like to live as part of an imperfect, and sometimes evil, community. We learn to pretend that we feel now what we cannot feel until heaven.

—Larry Crabb, *Inside Out*

I didn't feel at all hypocritical. I loved the Lord and I wanted to grow in that love. As God continued to work in my life, I was learning so much about being a Christian. I was excited, and everyone was happy for me. My Christian family loved and encouraged my enthusiasm, which was genuine. And never having had anyone love and care about me before, I wanted so desperately for them to continue loving me.

My fear was that if they really saw what was inside me, discovered who the real Carolyn Koons was, they wouldn't like me anymore. Maybe they wouldn't be so excited about who I was. Maybe they would back off, when they found out that a part of me was trash. So I kept my inmost burdens secret.

NAVIGATING THE INNER RAPIDS

All this time, I was growing in the Lord as an outgoing, energetic, young Christian. So that people wouldn't see the hidden part of me, my emotional barriers went up whenever I sensed someone trying to get a little too close. I still didn't trust people entirely. I had been hurt too many times. There remained in me a tough self, my way of fending people off and keeping them at a distance—far enough away that they couldn't see inside.

Some people seem to have X-ray vision, though, the ability to see right through us into those places of pain we keep hidden from everyone. Louie was certainly one of those people, at least where I was concerned. He seemed to know that I had a tough edge, that I wasn't about to let anybody get too close. So he started pressing the issue, an approach that might not be advisable with everyone but which was necessary in my case.

"Carolyn, why do you act so tough?" Louie challenged me one night. "What are you afraid of? Why won't you let anyone get close to you? Come on, Carolyn, let me in."

Terrified by his pressure and powered by instincts from my past, I smashed my fist right into Louie's face with a loud crack. POW! My knuckles landed squarely across the bridge of his nose! Louie's feet flew out from under him and he crashed to the ground. As he lay there, momentarily stunned, a small stream of blood burst from the bridge of his nose where my class ring had cut into his skin. I'm sure that he never expected me to deck him right there in church!

I was just as shocked at what I had done. *Oh, my God*, I thought, *I've hit Louie, and I love this guy! He meant the world to me, but now he's found out what I'm really like. It's all over. He'll never like me again!*

Louie regained his composure quickly. As he shook his head to clear it and jumped to his feet, his own first instincts possessed him momentarily. I could see his own rage as he pulled his fist back to strike. There we were, Carolyn Koons and her youth pastor, getting ready to duke it out in the church parking lot! Then Louie looked into my eyes where he could see the reflection of my fear and pain. He lowered his hands and stood there in silence.

I couldn't believe it. He didn't hit me! For the first time someone didn't hit back, and I didn't know how to take it. Of course, I was mortified. I wanted to die. I was so afraid that I had lost everything. But it was obvious Louie had forgiven me. He didn't reject me, even though he knew that something was troubling me deeply. I never wanted anything like that to happen again. I worked even harder to keep my secrets hidden, even from X-ray eyes.

The Bible says we are saved by God's love and God's grace, but it's also a fact that we're raised and taught by human beings. Some have taught us well and some others have not done such a good job. It has taken me years to learn that Christians in every avenue of life still have a lot of inner garbage, dead weight that they haven't either recognized, admitted, or dealt with. No matter what we have missed in our early years, God can make up for it in our adult life. But this is a lifelong process. I myself am still learning about the incredible power of God's healing.

The Bible says we are saved by God's love and God's grace, but it's also a fact that we're raised and taught by human beings.

I carried my personal crown of thorns with me wherever I went. I thought I carried it well, and didn't know how many people, if any, could see it. Louie had known, but he was a rare and perceptive friend. No one else talked with me the way he had.

If we hang on to the past, we may pay the price in anxiety, stress, pain, lost opportunities, desire for revenge, worthlessness, hopelessness, and despair. When we cling to unproductive memories or fantasies, we lack the energy and time for productive endeavors. Our self-image suffers because we focus on rejection, failure, and loss. We eventually may lose some of our friends, who may begin to tire of our constantly living in the past. When we hang on to the past, we are not free to grow, to accomplish our goals.

—Bobbie Reed, *Learning To Risk*

God continued to enrich my life. Becoming a Christian was the greatest thing that had ever happened to me, but I still bore those dry, piercing branches inside. I bore them carefully through that last year in high school. I brought them to college, to conferences, on mission trips, and into Christian ministry. I also wrapped and transported them, like bric-a-brac, to Azusa Pacific University where I became a faculty member, and even into the church where I eventually became the part-time minister in Christian education and youth work.

Carrying around this pile of brambles had become such a habit that most of the time I was unaware of it, but I carried that burden with me at all times, into my ministry, my relationships, into every area of my life.

UNCOVERING THE HIDDEN PAIN

On the campus of Azusa Pacific, as at all Christian colleges and institutions of higher learning across the nation, students are flooding into faculty and staff offices, seeking out the campus counseling centers, pouring out gut-wrenching stories of the suffering they have experienced. The kind of student walking onto the college campus today is a lot different than the student of fifteen or twenty years ago. Many are ready to express the ways in which abuse has touched their young lives, the personal tragedies which have led them to make rash and damaging choices about drugs and sex.

Too many of them were raised in alcoholic homes or experienced sexual abuse, enduring numerous tragedies that no young person should have to undergo. The ugliness they have known can be seen in the deep sadness in their eyes. A surprising number of these students make a bee-line to my office. It's as if they can sense that their pain once was mine.

On many occasions, I've sat with someone as the tears spilled out, mingled with intimate secrets, painful memories not far in the past. I recall Judy's torment. Her stepfather had held a large butcher knife to her throat as he prepared to rape her and threatened to kill her if she resisted.

I remember Kelly who told me that her father sexually molested her repeatedly during her years in junior high and high school. As if that weren't enough, her alcoholic mother beat her unmercifully and pulled out clumps of her hair. For days Kelly would cower in the basement of their home with all the lights out, her face so bloody and swollen that she didn't want anyone to see her. Her body was so bruised and aching, she couldn't move even to get food or water. Yet on campus, Kelley was outwardly a popular and ambitious student. Inside she was a violated child, deeply unhappy.

The physical abuse these two young women endured was almost beyond belief, and the emotional damage done to both was deep and debilitating. These tragic stories are not limited to women. Young Miguel was a handsome, well-built Cuban boy whom I had met and personally recruited for the university. After a few months of building trust, Miguel shared with me a horrific story of having been sexually abused by ranch hands on his father's tobacco plantation in Cuba, assaults which had been led by his cousin.

After his family fled Cuba to escape the powerful Castro regime, Miguel had become a Christian. His new life in Christ did not spare him from reacting to the pain of his past. Miguel was confused about his sexual identity and tormented by his behavior, which included an obsession for casual sex with predatory gay men. The abuse he'd suffered had left him with a habit of cruising the beach and inviting episodes of unsafe sex.

The issue wasn't whether Miguel was gay or straight, but that his past had polluted any notions about sexuality as an expression of a committed, healthy relationship. The abuse of earlier years had given this young man an ugly picture of sex as a mixture of brutality and animal gratification, and he couldn't seem to shake loose from its hypnotic hold.

Unfortunately, stories like Judy's, Kelly's, or Miguel's are all too common. Confidences such as these prompted me to begin work on a second master's degree in counseling at Talbot Theological Seminary. I remember the excitement I felt when I learned that I'd be taking a class in Counseling Techniques from one of the seminary's favorite professors and my good friend, Norm Wright.

The timing of this class couldn't be more perfect, I thought, since it would help me in reaching out to these students. Maybe I could get a handle on some of the deep issues they were facing.

Norm was a masterful teacher and his classes were always some of the most popular at the seminary. From the very first class period I was enthralled as he professionally and skillfully began to survey the field of counseling. I loved the course and took copious notes. That familiar yellow-lined paper began to fill my counseling notebook.

We weren't far into the course when Norm began to talk about the topic that most claimed my interest: today's abused, addicted society. He described the kind of people seeking out Christian counselors or walking into church doors today, people who were abused, damaged, and struggling with painful memories from their past. I can hear parts of his lecture in my mind as clearly as when I heard it in class for the first time.

"We all live with our memories of our past," Norm said, "and we are all products of our past. Each one of us is made up of a compilation of past experiences that we've brought with us into our adult life. These experiences are so powerful that they literally determine who we are, how we feel about ourselves, and what we will become in the future."

"You know," he continued, "that the origin, the seed of our self-image is derived essentially from the authority figures to which we submitted in our childhood. For most of us, the origin of our self-image lies mainly in our relationship with our parents. Other key authority figures in our lives during our childhood, such as a grandparent or aunt or uncle, also imprint our self-image. We may pick up some of our self-image from their input into our lives. But mainly, how we see ourselves depends upon what our parents reinforced for us."

My mind started racing like a state-of-the art computer, sorting out the consequences of what this psychologist had said. Suppose that when I was a child, my parents had told me I was the cutest, sharpest, smartest little girl in the whole world. Would I have grown up believing it? Would those positive and affirming words have become so integrated with my self-image that I would have acted from that conviction as I approached adulthood? With positive input from my parents, would I have developed a strong, confident inner picture of myself?

All such thoughts were mere conjecture. Truth was, my parents continually yelled at me and bombarded me with putdowns like, "That's stupid." Or worse, "You're stupid. Who do you think you are! You no good son of a bitch, you can't do anything right." According to this theory, I should have grown up believing and acting out those negative statements.

Norm went on to say that because our self-image was so deeply imprinted when we were little children, it is as if there is still a little child in us, regardless of our real age. Deep within, at the origin of who we are and how we feel about ourselves, there is still a little one, telling us what it believes to be true about ourselves.

Norm's words painted an increasingly disturbing picture. He showed us that in counseling people, we would be constantly dealing with shattered self-image issues, childhood issues, parent issues, and issues dealing with damaging memories. I had begun to suspect that he was talking not only about others, but about us! Whoa, I thought, this is powerful stuff! I glanced around the class to see if the other students were experiencing it as intensely as I was.

Norm then instructed each of us to put our notes to the side and to take out a clean sheet of paper. Large enough to take up the whole sheet, we were to draw a shield, like knights of old would have used in battle. We then drew a line vertically down the middle of the shield, dividing it in half, except for the bottom point. We finally drew three lines horizontally across the shield, which divided its surface into seven boxes of roughly equal size, depending on the shape of our shields.

We were now to label each of these boxes as containers for a certain age period of our lives. Starting at the top, upper left box, we moved across and down the shield and labeled each box in sequence: age one to six; seven to twelve; twelve to eighteen; eighteen to twenty-five; twenty-five to forty; forty to fifty-five; fifty-five and over. That was just the artwork; next came the exercise.

"OK class," Norm said with a jaunty air that clashed with my growing apprehension, "since psychologists say that our present behavior is continually being determined, patterned, and often controlled by our past memories and experiences, I would like you as potential counselors to begin to get in touch with some of your own past memories."

"I want you first to look at that part of the shield that represents ages one to six. Just let your mind begin to flow and reflect back to that time of your life. Whatever comes to your mind, whatever God brings to your mind, whether it is a wonderfully happy memory, or something painful, I want you to note it in some form on your shield. Write it out, draw stick figures, whatever, just put it on your shield so you can see it. You have the rest of the class time for this activity."

I looked at the clock and realized that Norm had given us well over half an hour. My first reaction was academic: how creative an exercise this was! I thought of ways I could modify it to identify leadership styles in a class I teach at APU. I enthusiastically grabbed my pencil and looked down at the neatly drawn shield.

But as I looked at the square representing the younger years, I felt a strange and uncomfortable feeling come over me. I stared at the shield but I couldn't seem to focus. My mind was racing, but moving in an aimless circle. I felt like I was watching an old TV when the vertical hold is broken, so that the grainy black-and-white picture keeps rolling endlessly. My heart began to pound and the palms of my hands began to get clammy. I simply couldn't think. I felt a powerful urge to panic, grab my books, and bolt for the nearest door.

I looked around the class and everybody else seemed to be diligently writing and drawing all kinds of stuff on their shields. I was the only one who was paralyzed. Norm quietly walked around the class, glancing over students' shoulders. I was frantically hoping he wouldn't come over to my seat, thankfully at the back of the room. My shield still lay in the desk in front of me, totally blank.

Finally, after ten to fifteen minutes had vanished, my anxiety was peaking. I had to start somewhere! I figured that the solution was to jump over the first three squares to ages eighteen to twenty-five and start from when I became a Christian. In that square on my shield I immediately drew a huge cross. Whew!!! Victory! Finally, I could breathe! Within a few minutes, I could feel my whole body begin to relax.

Underneath the cross, I drew a church. I drew little stick figures representing the youth group in our church, those who became my family and my world. The wonderful memories came spilling out on my paper as I drew symbols for the LA and San Pedro skid-row missions where the youth group served in the soup kitchen and held services. Next I drew little icons that represented the Mexico trips, the youth camp, the junior high youth group I sponsored, Azusa Pacific University, all the activities and ministries that had been part of my life with Christ.

To be honest, I could have taped six more sheets of blank paper next to those sections of the shield and filled them, too. After all, life began for me once I became a Christian. Anyone who says that they don't want to be a Christian because it's too confining or restrictive doesn't know the truth. Once I asked God into my life, an incredibly rich life opened for me, filled with wonderful experiences and adventures. I had both a purpose and a reason to wake up in the morning after I dedicated my life to God.

Norm eventually made his first pass along our back table. He stopped when he noticed that even though my shield was bulging with graphics, that the first half of my chart still remained very obviously blank. "Carolyn," he said, as he pointed his finger with authority at the blank portion of my shield, "make sure you fill in *all* of this chart."

I didn't look up at him, but instead halfheartedly nodded my head in agreement. I was surprised at my own reaction to his command. I felt resentment at his pressuring me. I began to think in my own defense, *This is just one of those make-work, useless little learning activities. I don't really have to do this. I mean, what's the big deal? I'm not going to fill in this chart. I don't need this anyway. This is for the rest of these students. After all, I'm a professor at another Christian university. I even teach classes here at Talbot. Just who does Norm think he's dealing with?*

Several more minutes passed, by the end of which the rest of the class had finished filling in their shields. The first half of my paper still lay pathetically blank, but I put my pencil down, folded my arms firmly, and set my jaw. I had done all that I was going to do. Norm made his second sweep past the back of my chair and again noticed my half-finished assignment. As his finger tapped me on the shoulder to get my attention, his voice sounded even more determined than before.

"Carolyn, I told you, I want you to fill in everything on your chart." Then, with an impish grin, he added, "The class will wait for you."

A sudden feeling of anger shot through my body, as it had those many years ago with my youth pastor. Once again, I felt the fingers on my right hand squeeze into a fist and my eyes blaze with a rage as sudden as a flash flood. I don't know quite what my face looked like, but my combativeness and anger prompted Norm to step back. Fortunately I put my fist down. I guess I'd learned something since the age of sixteen! The last thing I wanted to do was to get kicked out of seminary for decking my professor!

I was disarmed and confused about the whole incident. Norm was such a great teacher and good friend. As with Louie, I was so afraid that he would see that side of Carolyn Koons that I wouldn't let anyone see, and that maybe he wouldn't think so highly of me anymore.

All this from just a piece of paper! I grabbed my books and my purse and started for the classroom door. I wanted out of there, fast. Since classes were still in session, the wide hallway was completely empty as I darted through the seminary building. Halfway down the hall, my eyes welling with tears, I poured out my heart to God.

"OK, Lord," I prayed, "One of these days I am going to deal with this garbage.... One of these days, *but not now!* I have too much to do! There's our big Easter Mexico trip coming up in a few months, I'm working in a church, and I'm teaching full-time. I just don't have the emotional energy to deal with this stuff right now." I tried to hold God off, to keep him from uncovering the burden of my secret pain.

I could hardly wait to get far, far away from that threatening chart and into my car, to drive the forty minutes back to Azusa

Pacific University. I opened the car door, threw my books on the seat beside me and peeled out of the Talbot Seminary parking lot, back to the university, back to my womb of safety.

All the way there, I heard God's voice, whispering "When, Carolyn? When?"

I put the voice off. "Some day Lord, some day."

"But child," God seemed to say, in a tone much like Norm's chiding, "you have already been a Christian for eighteen years! *When are you going to deal with this garbage in your life?*"

FINDING THE PATH OF HEALING

"Jesus is in the business of forgiving and healing the past." I still remembered those simple words of invitation spoken by the evangelist, the message which had touched my soul as a teenager. Yet even in my thirties, I was still running from the grim realities I'd endured while growing up. I had become skilled at burying my past, but that no longer seemed to help. How could I live my life freely without putting all that pain somehow to rest? For that to happen, things would have to change inside.

If I had had the courage that day back in Norm's class, I might have drawn an ugly, black, thirty-eight-caliber gun. My childhood memory of that gun was too frightening and painful for me to share, but it had affected my whole life. I was eight years old when my mother walked into my bedroom, threw me up against the wall, and pointed my dad's fully-loaded pistol right at my face. Even though that terrifying incident happened over forty years ago, I can still see the rage on my mother's face. I can still see the bullets in the chamber of the gun. She had actually held her finger pressed tight against the trigger, the gun half-cocked. I felt that if I'd so much as breathed she would have blown my brains out right there!

"Carolyn!" she screamed, as she held that weapon of death inches from my head. "Your Dad hates you! He hates your guts! And one of these days he's going to kill you with this gun! You better pray that he dies before I die, because I'm the only thing that's keeping him from killing you!"

Only then did my mother drop the gun, the cold metal having served its purpose of driving the point home with a vengeance. Without another word, she stormed out of my bedroom and slammed the door behind her. I stood there against the wall for a long time, rigid with fear and unable to move.

The physical threat of becoming the victim of my father's insane, homicidal rages—kept white-hot by alcohol—did not end until he died. I remember him raging at me when I attended my grandfather's funeral. Dad made it crudely plain that he wished I'd never existed, that I didn't belong among the living mourners who'd gathered to pay respect. Shortly after that, he stalked me at my own home after having called the university switchboard with a death threat.

The police were powerless unless my father actually moved to carry it out. Knowing in my heart that his threat was real, I was left to deal with his murderous intentions. I still believe that my baby brother died as a result of one of his berserk and drunken episodes, and I considered it a miracle that I'd survived my childhood.

When I was a little girl, my father would typically come home from work so drunk that he would grab me, throw me on the kitchen floor, and hit me with his thick, leather belt or his fist, all the while screaming obscenities. The days I felt safest were those when he'd come home and pass out on the front porch. At least he couldn't hit me. In many ways, my mother was equally contemptuous of me, but when she said that she was the only thing standing between me and my father's desire to kill me, I believe she spoke the truth.

Even though certain people had been courageous and loving enough to alert me to my own pain, healing finally came to me as an adult through a very special blessing. My past had rendered me extremely suspicious of family intimacy. I never let people get too close. Then through a classmate and friend, I came to spend a weekend with a family up in the rural mountains of Twain Harte, California. Through their gentle and persistent love, Russell and Alva Peters eventually led me to accept their offer to be part of their extended family, which they proposed to me the very first night I spent under their roof.

Russell was a sensitive, godly pastor who consistently led his flock by his own Christian example. With four natural offspring and a number of foster children, his wife was a generous, open-hearted mother-figure to everyone. When I first met her, Alva's sincere warmth welcomed me in a way I had never experienced before. Their son Steven had been one of the most dynamic chapel speakers on campus as a student at Azusa Pacific. Students literally made pilgrimages to Twain Harte and to Chapel in the Pines where Russell was pastor. The church community, students, citizens of Twain Harte, and the Peters clan interacted like one huge and happy family. I have never seen such a natural and living community, before or since.

One afternoon at Twain Harte, Alva and I were standing in the hallway of the parsonage. We leaned against the doorjambs of opposite bedrooms and carried on a pleasant conversation. Then Russell came home and meandered down the hall to join us. As he raised his right arm to lean against the doorjamb, I saw his arm hover for an instant over my head. For an instant, I was caught in a shocking, intense flashback of my own father towering over me, his fist poised to come down on my neck or my face. With unconscious energy, I jumped back from the doorway, brought my arms in front of my body as if to defend myself, my fists ready to hit this kindly man of God!

Russell stood there with Alva, completely startled by my reaction. "Where did that come from?" Alva finally asked, after she had caught her breath.

"I don't know," I lied. I was so embarrassed at what I'd done. It was as if someone had turned the clock back fifteen years in a fraction of a second. I was a professor at a university, not some wild kid defying her youth pastor. Surely I didn't hit people still.

Russell responded with characteristic gentleness. He asked me point-blank, "Carolyn, when are you going to get some healing in your life?" Without another word, he walked to the living room, reached into the bookshelf, and took out a fairly small, obviously well-used paperback. "Carolyn, I want you to read this," he said. Then he placed in my hand a book that changed my life, *The Gift of Inner Healing*, by Ruth Carter Stapleton.

The bluntness of his question had stung me a little, but it had penetrated my defenses, too. As I rubbed my fingers on the worn pages of that book, I wondered how he'd known of the pain that lingered deep within me. I'd never told him anything about my past. I didn't need to, because Russell was another of those who could see right through me, into the recesses of my heart.

I was terrified by the potential of that book, or at least my inner demons were. It was not until some time later, when I had reason to believe that my father would actually carry out his threat of shooting me, that I opened its pages. Motivated by that greater terror, I thought that healing needed to come now or never.

As I sat in a lawnchair and began to savor that book, I let its pages suggest ways to bring healing to the damaged child that lay hidden from the world. Slowly, one by one, I called out the memories of the violence, the abandonment, the hatred that had marked my childhood, and asked the Lord Jesus to be present with me and heal them.

One of the biggest risks I've ever taken was that bright Saturday morning when I finally found the strength to open my spirit to Jesus and ask him to begin healing the pain of those memories. Jesus led me through each painful moment when the image of the gun had welled up in my life. As evening fell, my heart felt light for the first time in my life and I knew what it meant to be free! God had touched me with his love through that book and the love of Russell's whole family. I had come to know in my heart that forgiveness lies at the center of all inner healing.

One further ordeal yet remained. I experienced a nightmarish encounter with my father at my mother's funeral. With my son Tony's help, I had to give that gun once more into the Lord's hands. I remember arriving early at the pastor's study, where my father greeted me by grabbing my neck and shoving me onto a couch, snarling, "You son of a bitch. Sit there!" At the funeral, he manhandled me again, so that the entire ceremony became a blur, obscured by hurt and fear.

Strangely, as I prayed to erase the feelings that welled up from my father's crudity—even at the remembrance of my mother's death—I felt peace return to my heart and felt mostly pity for this man who had caused me so much pain. I knew then that healing had finally begun to come, and that it would be both deep and true. When I attended my father's funeral, the blessed *absence* of any anger or terror assured me that the threat of the gun was gone forever from my life.

Because I'm human and not perfect, I still harbor secret pain and I still have to work hard to overcome my fears. There was a time when I was afraid to let anyone see inside for fear that they wouldn't like me anymore. Over time that fear has vanished. But the more I've talked to people as I travel and speak, the more God has shown me that all of us have to deal with compacted garbage we've stored away for years, free (so we think) from prying eyes.

But I'm equally convinced from my own experience that sooner or later something will happen—a death, divorce, problems with children, finances, or the force of our own emotions—that will cause our carefully tied package to fly apart, exposing what's inside and carrying it on the wind like the evil spirits released from Pandora's box. If it's not a traumatic event that rends your heart, it may be the catalyst of meeting someone who sees your burden and doesn't judge you for it, but listens instead. Sometimes God will provide several such people, each of whom will move you a step closer to the healing you need.

Sharing our most painful memories and living with their awful truth weakens their hold over us. The process of healing, of transformation, truly begins.

Pain from dysfunction or abuse doesn't just stop one fine day. It goes on and on, as anyone who's grown up in such a home can tell you. The effects last a lifetime. In *Beyond Betrayal*, I relived the pain of my past again, and gained a new dimension of freedom. Embracing our stories, owning them without fear—whether in a confidential group setting, in a journal, or in prayer with God—is the first step to freedom and inner health.

Sharing our most painful memories and living with their awful truth weakens their hold over us. The process of healing, of transformation, truly begins. One day, as I can testify, the process will be completed, finished, or as Jesus said on the cross, "consummated." As the burden of pain is lifted, you will be free to move along life's course, to taste all of its thrilling adventures without fear.

CHAPTER 9

Help for the Journey

To the novice traveler, fresh from
the protection of a familiar home, a
changing, alternating mode will be
difficult. So it's going to take practice; and when learned the new
behavior will in itself be just as
steady and stable as it was before.

Don Koberg and Jim Bagnall,
The All New Universal Travel Guide

Over the last thirty years I've
talked with scores of
Christians whose lives are stuck, whose painful past weighs them
down and makes it impossible for them to move on. I've listened
to heartbreaking tales of abused childhoods, alcoholic homes, sexual abuse, abandonment, betrayal. Many of these emotionally
damaged believers seem to be paralyzed by chronic weariness.

Christ assured his disciples that "my yoke is easy and my burden
is light." So what keeps each of us from lightening our load? My
own deepest inhibition has always been resistance to looking
inside. If I *were* to take an honest look at the whole of my life,
maybe I wouldn't be able to handle it. Sound familiar? Once we

turn the spotlight on ourselves, we realize why owning our secret pain is such a risk. Our very identity is on the line, or at least the precious self-image we project for all the world to see.

Will exposure mean that we'll fall apart emotionally? Won't other people think less of us? Could it be that this wonderful God in whom we believe wouldn't be willing to help us through such dark terrain? Would looking inside be so painful that we'd lose our faith? All these doubts and more give us incentive to deny our pain and wrap our secrets even more tightly.

A choice made several times becomes a habit. A habit practiced long enough becomes a lifestyle. A lifestyle becomes a footprint in the sand anyone can see, a track that reveals who we've become, for better or worse. The scars and dark memories that make up part of everyone's past can help to explain some of the experiences which have made us who we are today. So many times, they can also act as an anchor that pins us firmly to one spot in the river.

Once that anchor has been firmly planted by repeated choices, we find it very difficult to cut the rope and float free. Such a decision means relinquishing a part of ourselves, even though it's not a part we necessarily cherish. Over time, even pain becomes familiar and healing a cause for fear. We often feel a strong inner resistance to getting the help we need.

A choice made several times becomes a habit.
A habit practiced long enough becomes a lifestyle.
A lifestyle becomes a footprint in the sand anyone
can see, a track that reveals who we've become,
for better or worse.

Even if we know that counseling would be the best investment for our time and money, we still tend to play that old game of waiting for our schedule to clear and our budget to change—as if by some will of their own. When they don't, we have built another barrier to change from the elastic substance known as denial.

God promises complete healing, provided that we offer him our whole selves without reserve. Yet we all try to keep part of our-selves hidden, like Adam and Eve trying to conceal their original sin. When they heard God approaching in the cool of the evening, our first parents hid in the garden and tried to cover their naked-ness. The knowledge of good and evil gained by their disobedi-ence made them feel embarrassed and exposed, guilty and fearful. Adam and Eve tried to cover their sin by covering their bodies, to hide their shame and fear and seal themselves off from God's dis-cerning gaze.

How many times do we walk through life just like that, con-cealing the source of our own shame and hoping that God won't notice? The desire to deny, to keep the lid on tight, is observable everywhere. We live in a society plagued with pressures, addiction, violence, and abuse. That's what it means to live in a fallen world. Small wonder people are confused, scared, wounded, even destroyed. Sometimes it is because of something they did, yet more often the root cause is something that happened to them.

Let us not be so naïve to think that the pain inflicted by society stops at the door of the sanctuary. Wounded people have been flocking into our churches for years.

It's easy to call pain a social problem and to overlook the very personal damage done to people's souls. Let us not be so naïve to think that the pain inflicted by society stops at the door of the sanctuary. Wounded people have been flocking into our churches for years. They come seeking help, someone to listen, answers to their questions. They want to know if there is any reason to be alive. Today more than ever, the church is feeling the impact of society's ills.

Christians stand at the threshold of decision. Are we going to wake up and respond to these life issues and to these hurting peo-ple? Or will we bow our heads so we won't see the hurt? Will we sing a little louder in the hope that it will go away? Let's look at some vital strategies for breaking down the barriers to change, for embracing the broken-hearted, for receiving and sharing God's healing love and forgiveness.

BUILD HONEST COMMUNITY

Many believe that in order to enter the church, they must leave their pain at the door. I'll never forget the first time I saw a Christian in obvious pain. Cynthia was all but a local legend in youth ministry when I met her for the first and only time. I had come to a neighboring church for a planning session in preparation for a city-wide Youth Extravaganza with Wes, our church's Minister of Christian Education, and Louie, our Youth Pastor. As we pulled into the parking lot, they spotted a well-dressed, vibrant young woman walking with a brisk step into the church.

"Hey, Cynthia's here!" Wes exclaimed. "She's the greatest! If she's going to help with the planning, this event will be great!" I was impressed with the enthusiasm this woman had been able to spark on sight. Someone else remarked that Cynthia was over thirty and never married, which was far from where I wanted to be when I got to that "ripe old age." Then the conversation began to shift as Wes and Louie shared their concern.

"Cynthia's sure been going through some tough times these past couple years," Louie said. "She lost both her parents in a car accident and it really hit her hard. She dropped out of ministry for about a year and a half after that. She was the key person for youth and Christian Ed in this area, but this is the first time I've seen her back for a meeting."

"I understand there've been problems more recently," Wes added. "I can understand how she intimidates church leadership. She's talented, dynamic, creative, probably one of the best administrators you'll ever meet. But I hear she's resigned from her church for personal reasons, and I think there are emotional and financial problems, too."

Wes and Louie got out of the van and went over to greet Cynthia at the church door. They shared a long hug. Then I saw Cynthia's head drop, as her whole body language changed from one of confident energy to a darker dialect of pain. It was evident to anyone that these old friends were having a very difficult conversation, and that Cynthia stood in deep need of their comfort and support.

In the excitement of the day, I forgot about Cynthia for a while. When I finally thought to look for her at the meeting, I discovered that she hadn't come into the church after all. I never saw this woman again, nor did I ever know what happened to her, but she made an enormous impression on me. Cynthia's face pops into my mind often when I'm at prayer. She was the first Christian I'd known who had moved away from the church when she was most in need of its support.

---

*Many believe that in order to enter the church,
they must leave their pain at the door.*

I remember other revelations from that day—the fact that jealousy could rear its head among church leaders, that a loving family could turn its back on pain it wasn't prepared to understand, that Christian women could pursue goals other than marriage and family. I learned that my idealistic image for my life was too pat, and that it might be subject to some radical change. I began to see that there might well come a time when I could be so overwhelmed by pain that what I'd need most was not another inspirational event, but a simple hug, offered with support and genuine love.

I myself had come into the church wounded, lonely, confused, and angry. I wasn't alone then, and times haven't changed. People all around us are scared, hurting, lonely, cast adrift. Their individual lives are falling apart, their families are being destroyed, and they are crying for help. The people walking into today's churches are often seeking help to put their shattered lives and dreams back together. Perhaps that describes your own state of heart, either now or when you first decided to give your life to God.

At long last, the church is waking up and beginning to address the very human pain of its membership. More than ever within the body of Christ, Christians are finding the support, encouragement, and guidance they need to continue their journey. When all goes well, church life serves all at once as a sturdy raft, a strong and exciting current, and a clear map for life.

One of the hidden costs I pay for traveling and speaking virtually every weekend is that I've lost the support and connectedness I once enjoyed through active church membership. Yet I also see a bright side of visiting a different throng of believers each week. I have witnessed first-hand the amazingly creative, relevant ways in which needs are being addressed—divorce recovery groups, singles groups, single-parenting groups, adult children of alcoholics groups, support groups for victims of sexual abuse, support groups for adults with aging parents.

Healing comes when those whose lives are fragile mingle with those who have found strength to celebrate life again. In good times and bad, we need to share our journey with fellow believers who know and love us. The church is summoning its courage to face the reality of human imperfection with ancient but effective weapons of prayer, grace, and forgiveness, as well as seeking to incorporate new ways to surmount barriers to human wholeness.

At long last, the church is waking up and beginning to address the very human pain of its membership.

TAKE ONE STEP AT A TIME

Life in Southern California is a little like its freeway system—always go, go, go. Everywhere you can see people in a frenzy of activity, at work, at play, or just getting from place to place. One old joke about this part of the country is that if it isn't moving at fifty-five miles per hour, it doesn't exist! Slowing down seems like a heavenly idea, but how can we possibly do it if we're used to such a frantic pace?

Four summers ago, I scheduled time to rest and write. I never did either one, by my own choice. At the end of that summer I was *still* saying, "When my schedule clears up, I'm going to put my feet up, set my laptop computer on my lap for once, and express myself." Of course, that would have meant exchanging my chosen lifestyle for one that was less hectic and distracting. I guess at some level, I wasn't willing to take the risk.

How many times have you said to yourself, "When my schedule clears up, I'm going to take that class... teach myself Spanish... read the stack of books on my nightstand... take a *real* vacation for a change... go on a diet... spend more time with God's Word... give up chocolate... "? When will "when" ever come? How about today?

What keeps us from moving on? Truly implementing any of these resolves would mean inviting change into our lives. Like beavers working hard to build a dam, keeping busy is one of the barriers we build in order to avoid cascading into unknown waters. Several other very effective barriers can hold us in place at a certain point on life's river. I have built most of these barriers at some point in my own life.

Impatience often holds us back. Our inordinate desire to be at the end of the journey can stop us before we even take the first step. When faced with the prospect of a painful journey, we often search for a short cut, an easy way out that will eliminate the need to take all the steps. Because we want the pain of transition to go away (sometimes even before we experience it), we aren't willing to spend the time it takes to effect real change in our lives.

Fear of the unknown is yet another barrier to necessary change.

Fear of the unknown is another barrier to necessary change. Maybe what we don't know can't hurt us, but it certainly can paralyze our progress. What if I fail in my quest? What if I end up alone? How could I bear the loss of money, security, or precious time? Fear of flying blind into the future, even to find our real selves and our true purpose, can keep us from receiving God's best gift.

Even our best intentions can be sabotaged by *poor priorities.* "One step at a time" is the watchword of Alcoholics Anonymous, but it's vital advice for any and every journey toward recovery and wholeness. The future seems overwhelming when we believe that we must conquer the world all at once. We easily become confused and discouraged when we try to consider the rest of our lives. In order to be nourished by our own future, we need to break it into manageable bites. At every decision point, I find it helpful to ask these four questions:

- What shall I do?
- What shall I choose not to do?
- What shall I do first?
- What shall I do next?

Sometimes a *lack of vision* can stop us in our tracks. We can visualize God's will for us as lying behind either a closed door or an open door. We can slide to a halt before barriers of our own devising, or we can look for opportunities, decide to thrive and grow, and create a dream. What do you want to experience in your life? Who would you like to become?

Press on to answer those questions. As my colleague Harold Ivan Smith has often said, "Appreciate your dream. It deserves a chance!" Or as we read in Scripture, "With God, all things are possible." You can survive anything with his help. Don't give up. Continue to take it one step at a time, even if it is only a tottering baby step. Discover all you are created to be by saying yes to change.

FOLLOW AN EXPERIENCED GUIDE

There have been many times when skies have darkened in my life, many of which have come since I became a Christian. For example, I faced incredibly dark days getting my son Tony out of that Mexican prison. More stormy times followed as I learned painful lessons about how to mother an abused child.

I vividly remember one day when Tony had acted out in some spectacular way. I prayed in utter frustration, "God, what have you done to me? I asked you to *change* my life, not *ruin* it! You gave me a son, and I can't even stand to be in the same room with him! It's not fair!" I've learned since that few parents have not prayed this prayer (usually many times over), whenever they felt that the impossible job of parenting had led them to the end of their rope.

Loneliness, a feeling especially well-known to singles, has led to some pretty gloomy hours in my life as well. Like most other people, I have also felt the need of sunlight in my life as I wrestled with work-related problems, relationship difficulties, physical illness, and the sadness of being disappointed or rejected.

Whether we cry out to the Lord in frustration and pain, or seek his face in times of deep loneliness and questioning, God is the best possible guide for navigating life's river. Knowing him has given me the confidence to face seemingly impossible situations. Who better than life's Creator to show us the way? We are God's creation, and that means he can unlock any mystery that stands in our path.

Psalm 100 sings out this truth joyfully and well: "Know that the Lord is God. It is he who made us, and we are his; we are his people, the sheep of his pasture." Saints through the ages have discovered that the destination of life is to know God and enjoy him forever. God is the divine Guide who loves us and never leaves us.

The proofs of God's loving presence are all around me every minute of every day. My Creator has helped me reach my potential in so many areas. He has led me to wonderful friends with whom I delight in sharing my journey. God also led me to adopt my son Tony, an incredible part of my journey in itself. Through his leading, I began the Mexico Outreach Program at APU with sixty students, and have seen that number grow to thousands.

Again, Psalm 100 helps me to find words of thanks for all that God has shown me of his creation, and for the courage he has given me to travel the river of life: "Enter his gates with thanksgiving and his courts with praise; give thanks to him and praise his name. For the Lord is good and his love endures forever; his faithfulness continues through all generations."

Whether we cry out to the Lord in frustration and pain, or seek his face in times of deep loneliness and questioning, God is the best possible guide for navigating life's river.

In addition, millions of God's children who have gone down the river before us can now serve as helpful guides to those of us who need help. We read about many of them in the pages of Scripture, in biographies, in the daily news, or through stories passed down to us by family or friends. Some are celebrities—saints and even a sinner or two—but still ordinary people have left valuable information along the riverside, hoping we will stop long enough to study their legacy and learn from it. Like a map to buried treasure stuffed in the hollow of a tree, their life stories are a gift to help prepare and guide us in our own journey through life. If we take the time to heed their experience, we won't have to go down the river quite so blindly.

At times, special people have given us personal direction. They may have swum to the side to free us from our death grip on the riverbank, or stayed with us in the raft when the water suddenly became rough. Some of these people we've intentionally pursued, while others appear to have been sent by God. Personal guidance on the river may come in the form of messages preached by our pastors and priests. We could all benefit from the insight of spiritual directors and the help and support offered by Christian counselors and therapists, people who are especially gifted and trained to lead and guide us through difficult life passages.

Whenever a guide touches another person's life for good, one more individual is enabled to get unstuck and move toward mainstream. When I reflect on my life, I always recall with gratitude the people who helped to guide its course. We're connected by the strong bonds of memory which strengthen me at my core. Louie, my youth pastor who hung in there until he thought I could survive without him, offers one example. I was right off the streets when I came to his youth group. To me, it seemed that Louie knew everything about the Christian life, while I knew nothing. He helped me through more rapids than you could shake a paddle at!

I knew that Louie was taking a lot of flack for the work he was doing with me and some of the other tough kids in our youth group. "Don't waste your time on that one, Louie," some people would say. "She's too hardened and tough. Spend more time with the other kids. They won't give you so much trouble." But Louie told them (and later told me), "Carolyn isn't too tough for me. I'm not giving up on her because she's going to make a difference in her world." I thank God for Louie and his willingness to be a guide for those who had wandered off the path.

Wes was another such person in my life. He was a minister of Christian education and music and one of the most creative, energetic people I have ever met. I was still a young Christian when Wes came alongside to lend a helping hand and steady my wobbly raft. His was the Sunday School class into which I walked, attitude and all, the very first time I set foot in the church.

As Wes taught at youth rallies attended by hundreds of kids, we found the courage to look at our lives. Each time I listened to him, I was able to give God just a little more of myself. I could sense that the process was changing my life. Wes believed in me, and he trusted the God he taught me to trust. His excitement about ministry, about Christian education and youth work, about the church in general, and most of all about the people to whom he ministered, instilled in me the desire to work in the field of Christian education.

I must have been a pretty tough nut to crack, because God sent so many people into my life to show me the way—not the least of whom was Al. A tall and gangly, mild-mannered sort of guy, smiling Al never failed to engage my spirit. His passion for missions was equally engaging, I soon discovered. Al was a youth pastor in a church near the one I attended and had organized a trip into the interior of Mexico. Many of us saw and experienced things on that trip that changed our lives forever.

It didn't take Al long to recognize my hidden administrative gifts and put me to work helping him organize these ministry trips. His vision to involve people in ministry soon became my own. As soon as I went to Azusa Pacific University, I began to organize student outreach trips every holiday break. Now I direct the university's Institute for Outreach Ministries. We take thousands of people of all ages on ministry trips all over the world, seeing and sharing life-changing experiences. I hope that ministry will be seen as part of my gift of guidance for others.

CHART YOUR COURSE

After my second rafting trip, I concluded that there had to be a better way to get down the river. Maybe I could commandeer a battleship and protect myself entirely. That would be formidable and safe, but not much fun! Maybe I could take a speedboat over the top of the rapids or perhaps tie weights to my ankles, strap a scuba tank to my back, and trust myself to the current's mercy! Then again, I could wait until the river dried up and just walk down the dry river bed.

My imagination suggested all kinds of options, but the one I resisted the longest was really the most practical. Why hadn't I just gone to the U.S. Forest Service and gotten a map? Then I would have been prepared for the difficult places in the river. I don't think I was stubborn; I just didn't think I needed help! It wasn't until I crashed on the river the second time—and had to pay for the harpooned raft which I had borrowed—that I began to see the wisdom in getting hold of a map to the river.

I discovered, belatedly, that this is in fact the correct way to go white-water rafting. You are *supposed* to go to the Forest Service *before* you brave the river! After all, their job is to study the river on behalf of those who want to travel it. These professionals are acquainted with all its features, including its dangers, with up-to-date information on the river's shifting peculiarities and daily conditions.

To make sure that the river is safe for you and me, the Forest

Service assigns experts to test the waters and to chart the best course. In any season, they know the height of the water flow based on recent rain and snow accumulations. Their detailed river maps are ours for the asking. Just by looking at these masterpieces, you can learn what conditions lie ahead in each section of the river and what to expect in the way of hazards.

These maps even rank the severity of each set of rapids on a scale of one through six, from the simplest of rapids to the ones to be avoided at all costs. They recommend that everyone be checked out beforehand in order to know their level of ability. This river-ranking then helps them stay within their skill limits. Rafters proceed up to the next ranking only after they've been carefully trained and prepared for more treacherous encounters. Now they tell me! If we had paid attention to the masters of the river, we would have heeded their warning not to go near a hazard ranked number six.

God has also provided maps which have been wisely and carefully prepared to help all of us to negotiate every obstacle that lies ahead on the journey. We could never anticipate all the joys and disappointments, the wonderful gifts and painful tragedies, the blessings and trials that stretch across each lifetime.

God has also provided maps which have been wisely and carefully prepared to help all of us to negotiate every obstacle that lies ahead on the journey.

Sometimes these maps are not obvious; we have to make some effort to seek them out. It is more than worth the search. Other times the guide charts are right in front of our eyes, but we have become so accustomed to plotting our own course that we can't even see them. It is up to us to discover both the hidden and obvious helps, and then to devour their data much like Jeremiah ate the scroll of prophecy. As we do, we are enabled to face our journey with confidence and power and wisdom.

Sometimes we're more focused and intentional about charting

the course of our lives, but many times we tend to be fairly hap-hazard—just going with the flow, floating downstream, passive and unprepared, at the mercy of every current. We can feel rather helpless, not knowing what lies ahead, when suddenly that unexpected pothole in the river engulfs us. We sink deeper and deeper, weighted by despair. Swamped, overwhelmed, and resentful, we feel trapped. An old refrain quickly rises up within us: *Why is this happening to me? It all seemed so easy just a short while ago. I knew it was too good to be true!*

Being prepared for the river enables us either to avoid the hazards or shoot through them so we won't get trapped and sucked under, unable to finish the journey.

If we give our journey enough forethought, we will let go of our expectations for smooth sailing. We will be prepared to face some rough sections of the current in order to reach our destination. Preparing ourselves for the journey means knowing where those sections of white water are located. Being prepared for the river enables us either to avoid the hazards or shoot through them so we won't get trapped and sucked under, unable to finish the journey.

While no one is ever entirely prepared for adult life, there is really no excuse to go through life ignorant and oblivious to barriers, hazards, and zones of safety. The maps are available, ours for the taking. Life maps can both direct us to some spectacular sights and save us a lot of grief, if we are serious about studying them.

The life maps that are available to us come in many forms, but the greatest map to the river is our personal relationship with God. God is the One who has our whole life's map in front of him. He also makes himself available to guide us wisely through all of its course. God personally and skillfully maneuvers us through the myriads of experiences in this adventurous journey.

God has also provided us with a map which is always readable, no matter what the light. That's because it has a light of its own. The Holy Scriptures, the Word of God, has lit my path when it seemed darkest and reminded me that I am safe in God's everlasting arms. Next to my personal relationship with God through Jesus Christ, the Bible has helped me the most to plan and surmount the dark times of my life. Within its pages is the map that leads us to eternal life, with secrets to this life recorded in abundance and deciphered for the heart by the Holy Spirit.

The Bible can help us to find the comfort and courage we need to move down the river. Ask yourself how much time you honestly spend reading God's Word. In the Bible, we've been given the most precious map imaginable; we all need to seek its guidance more often. When we reach the end of our energy, resources, and skills, and call out to God in prayer, the Holy Spirit will lead us and show us the way through those sacred pages.

The Word of God will beckon to you. If you respond and read it, the importance of its wisdom will deepen and begin to make sense in new ways, as God moves from your head to rest in your heart. You will experience not a fleeting happiness that comes and goes according to your circumstances, but a deep and abiding joy.

The Scriptures are filled with valuable information, truths, warnings, and promises to help us down this river called life. Yet at the end of his Gospel, the apostle John says that Jesus did and taught so many things "... If every one of them were written down, I suppose that even the whole world would not have room for the books that would be written" (Jn 21:25). How true! More than ever before, Christian writers are extending the truths of the Bible to give hurting, stuck people maps to help them get through the narrow, chaotic channels of life.

I know how meaningful and lifegiving such books can be. When I first became a Christian, I felt tremendously blessed to know that Jesus was caring for my broken heart. I wanted the presence of God to fill me completely so that I could experience a deeper walk with God. Someone gave me a book by Major Ian Thomas, entitled *The Abundant Life of Christ*. The Spirit-filled wisdom woven into these pages brought me to that deep and rich relationship with God I'd so fervently sought.

A book can be like a map of someone's journey down a part of their river, whose twists and turns look much like our own. This commonality gives the written word power to guide and change your life. I have listed some of these helpful books in a small bibliography at the end of this book. One that I want to take special care to mention is Richard Foster's excellent *Celebration of Discipline,* another book which had a strong impact on my spiritual life. As you read these books or others in your personal library, you may come to learn something about yourself or about life that will help you plan your course more purposefully.

It took me much longer to discover navigational aids to the river of life than to locate the maps to actual rivers. The alternative approach is to study the river first-hand. Studying the river gives us more confidence and power. If we're alert, there are many things on the river that will give our senses a treat, from the music of the rushing water to the smell of aspen and pine, to the sights of unspoiled nature. Of course, in order to enjoy all of this natural beauty, we need to be watchful. Being prepared for the rough places in life is far preferable to dropping deep into the vortex of an emotional breakdown before we ever realize that we need help.

God intends for us to appreciate the beauty and joy in creation, and to come together as a community both to celebrate the journey, as well as to find the healing and strength we need to move down the river and experience its wonders. When we do, we often discover one of the great gifts to God's people—*the gift of music.*

I have found that foot-tapping, hand-clapping, soul-zapping music can bring you close to God faster than practically anything else. It's also a special kind of map. Music countless times has caused me to feel God's nearness again when I'd lost that sense of his presence. When I get away from God, I lose my way so quickly. When I hit one set of rapids after another, not only do I get knocked around, I get cold, and then I grow numb. Numbness is not only dangerous, it's an unnatural state. Real people feel, and music pours feeling back into numb bodies and paralyzed souls.

When it comes to inspiring music, I am at a particular advantage at Azusa Pacific University. Three times a week we celebrate in chapel and it has become for me the highlight of the week's activities. When eighteen hundred students sing together, it sounds to me like a choir of angels. I feel like God is there singing with us, maybe in the chair right next to me! Good things well up in my heart; I feel in tune with my Savior. Songs of praise lift me up like nothing else, and I feel as if I'm walking along a bridge of song that links my soul to God. Music is often God's way of pointing the way up through the accumulated garbage that blocks my path to him, so that I, too, can sing his praises.

Giver of life, creator of all that is lovely,
    Teach me to sing the words to your song;
I want to feel the music of living
    And not fear the sad songs
But from them make new songs
    Composed of both laughter and tears.

Teach me to dance to the sounds of your world and your
    people,
    I want to move in rhythm with your plan,
Help me to try to follow your leading
    To risk even falling
    To rise and keep trying
Because you are leading the dance.
            —Tim Hansel, *Choosing Joy*
            (original author unknown)

PREPARE FOR RISKS

On many of my rafting adventures, I was the one who should have known the dangers of the river. As the one in charge, I should have gone to the Forest Service and obtained a river map in order to stay clear of insurmountable dangers. I'm not suggesting that studying a map to the river would have taken the risk out of rafting. It just makes sense that in minimizing the risk, we maximize the potential for enjoyment.

Risks are essential to living out the promises of life.

We need to distinguish the difference between taking healthy risks and living recklessly. Risks are essential to living out the promises of life. The children of Israel provide a perfect example of people who were afraid to risk. Instead of making a beeline to the promised land, they wandered in the desert for forty years. Most of that time they complained that life had been better in Egypt, where things were at least more predictable and the meals were more regular.

The Israelites were called by God to take a risk and to move forward, but it was very difficult for them to get unstuck. I like to think that if I were an Israelite, I would have been pushing Joshua and Caleb into the promised land, eager to gorge myself on milk and honey for the rest of my life. But would I really have been willing to take *any* risk to claim that inheritance? I can only hope so, because God calls me forward to the promised land in the same way today.

In contrast to accepting risk, living recklessly is simply foolish. We can end up sabotaging our lives when we disregard our priorities. People who live from the "outside in" are living recklessly. They react to external situations and popular opinion rather than listening and responding to God within. People who use drugs or abuse alcohol are consigned to a life of recklessness—their lives controlled by a need that takes priority over everything else and must be satisfied, whatever the cost.

Recklessness takes different forms. It can be reckless to disregard wise counsel or your doctor's advice. It is certainly reckless to spend more money than you have. Sexual promiscuity is reckless, especially in an age which knows the tragic reality of AIDS. It can even be reckless to work so hard that you forget to play, or to become so playful that life loses a sense of serious purpose.

Risks, on the other hand, make life interesting. I'm not sorry for the risks I've taken. I love to match my skill and courage to a task that is just beyond my reach. As I stretch to meet this new challenge, I grow and change.

We have seen the need for exploring the landscape of the riverside and perhaps pausing there from time to time to regain our strength. Rather than overstay our welcome and become stuck, however, we also need to risk a return to the river once our issues have been resolved and our energy replenished. Stuck people die a little every day. People in the river are going places and growing.

A reflective essay on aging contains the following remarks, written by an eighty-five-year-old who is still growing. Speaking with wisdom rather than regret, she shares what she would do differently if she had to live her life all over again: "I'm one of those persons who never goes anywhere without a thermometer, a hot water bottle, a raincoat and a parachute. If I had it to do again, I would travel lighter than I have.... I would take more chances, I would climb more mountains and swim more rivers. I would eat more ice cream and less beans. I would perhaps have more actual troubles, but I'd have fewer imaginary ones."

What this woman reveals is the lesson life would teach us all: don't shy away from risk. We need to take the necessary risks to continue our journey. Some people must endure chemotherapy, undergo radical surgery, enter rehabilitation centers, or join recovery groups—all of these are choices some people must make in order to live. No guarantees are handed out at the door, but the risk is worth it.

Today, some individuals are finding the courage to put a stop to an abusive relationship. While representing a huge risk, such a step may be necessary just in order to survive, but also to regain quality and hope for life. Others of us decide to go back to school, change careers, or have a baby after the age of forty. It's impossible to stay in the river and keep moving on without taking risks.

But the river of life is hard enough without ignorance of the known hazards making it harder. When we begin our journey as infants, we are totally dependent and can't read the maps—like Moses, who was on a journey not of his choosing. We're all set upon the river of life the minute we're born. After some years, God gives us the capability to take objective stock of life and to plan our course. Doesn't it just make sense to get a good map and study it thoroughly?

It sounds so simple, so comforting, and yet, the shores of life are crowded with stuck people who don't know that they have that capability. Perhaps like me, you awakened one morning well into your adult life and suddenly realized that you didn't feel prepared for life. The rapids were too crazy. Life was a bigger challenge than you ever expected. Thankfully, that realization has come and gone for me. I have accepted responsibility for my life. I am now capable of getting a map and reading it. I wish the same for everyone.

All of us reach adulthood with a few holes in the fabric of our upbringing that make us feel helpless or needy. Along the way, a stitch was dropped here and there, probably because someone was busy just trying to survive. So within the pattern of our adult life, childish patterns re-emerge. We whine when we're tired, we become angry or silly when we're embarrassed, and we react to unexpected things in life as if we were helpless children, unable to spot them on the map.

Our consternation is partly because we assume we're prepared just because we have managed to reach the age of adulthood. We suppose through some magic that we've learned enough to be considered pros. Somewhere on the river it finally dawns on us that we didn't know as much about life as we thought. That first seemingly unbearable experience comes smashing into our lives, churning our preconceptions into a froth and throwing us into despair and depression. What seems like a tidal wave may smack us so hard that we lie momentarily stunned. Somehow, we make it through. We often don't even know how.

We don't respect the rapids until we hit them. Then our confidence weakens, because we hoped that somehow we would be that charmed exception to the dangers and tragedies in life. We continue on downriver, wondering when the next patch of white water will hit, and asking ourselves, "Is this what the rest of the journey is going to be like?"

Did you expect God to exempt you from trials because of your faith in him? Like me, did you feel that God loved you in such a special way that he would protect you from the pain everyone must feel, or find others to bear it for you? No, God has promised to accompany us on our journey, not to remove us from the journey.

> *God has promised to accompany us on our journey, not to remove us from the journey.*

It will take far less time than "threescore years and ten" to encounter most of the hazards and barriers life has to offer. We will need the wisdom of many guides, along with the help of every map God can provide. But when we choose to navigate the river, to grow, and to take responsibility for our lives, we can expect God to be there with us, to give us continued courage to stay unstuck and to move on.

CHAPTER 10

Five Steps
to Freedom

> Too often, vision is seen as emerg-
> ing primarily from a charismatic
> leader or a ruling elite. But if we
> sincerely believe God speaks to all
> members of a body of believers,
> then we need to discover ways to
> find the vision God is giving every-
> one in that body.
>
> Tom Sine, *Wild Hope*

A few years ago, I came across an article by Warren H. Schmidt, Chair of the Economy and Efficiency Commission. Entitled "Two Paths to the Future," it was a parable about a time much like our own, a time of great turmoil and confusion, when the winds of change were often violent and unpredictable.

Dr. Schmidt's parable describes how people gathered in two groups to confront the shock of change. One group was called the *Predictors of the Inevitable*. These people said, "Let's be realistic. Things have gotten out of control and the ordinary person is pow- erless to change it." Wherever the Predictors' voices dominated, the results were fairly predictable: people became apathetic and cynical; innovation and hope were silenced; and helplessness became the only reality. The Predictors could then say truthfully, "We told you so."

The second group was called the *Pursuers of the Possible.* They faced their fears of the future with confidence, both in themselves and in those around them. They always had hope; their word to everyone who proposed to act was "Try!" The Pursuers listened and were willing to work together to create solutions, rather than dwell in the shadow of their problems. Not surprisingly, wherever the Pursuers held sway, people came alive with excitement and hope and began to act as if they had the power to shape their future. As they acted, their vision cleared, their strength increased, and their confidence grew.

The Pursuers were never as impressive at foretelling the future as the Predictors, but they discovered a great truth, which Dr. Schmidt shares on behalf of Pursuers of the Possible everywhere: "It is better to test your strength and be wrong than proclaim your weakness and be right, for it is far less heroic to fulfill a prophecy of despair than to fail while pursuing a dream of hope."

Let me tell you another story which speaks to this same issue of how a lack of creative and perceptive spirit stifles the expressive side of life. It recounts what happened to a college professor on one of those golden, autumn days when you feel drawn to step outside and drink in the universe. James Smith, a member of the education faculty at State University of New York at Oswego, was gathering his easel, paints, and brushes for a day of painting in a nearby meadow.

When he saw his young daughter peeping in at the doorway, he invited her to come along. Together they started off, down a long hill and through the soft grasses of the meadow to the edge of a deep blue lake. Fortunately for us, Smith is also a writer who is sensitive to all of life's images. He writes:

On the lake, a single white sailboat tipped joyously in the breeze. My daughter looked up and claimed it. She painted with abandonment and concentration. Before I had really begun, she pulled a painting off her easel. "There!" she said. "Want to see?"

I cannot describe the sense of wonder that flowed through me as I viewed her work. It was all there. She had captured the sunlight in her spilled yellows, the lake in her choppy, uneven strokes of blue, the trees in her long fresh strokes of green. Through it all there was a sense of scudding ships and the joyousness of wind that I experience when I sail, the tilting and swaying of the deck, the pitching of the mast. It was a beautiful and wondrous thing.

His daughter called this work of art "Sailboats," even though not a single sailboat appeared in her picture. Smith framed it and proudly hung it on the wall. The sad part of the story began when she started school the following week. She came home from school and asked her father to help her draw a picture of a sailboat. "Why, sweetheart," he said, pointing to her September artwork on the wall, "I could never paint a picture like the one over there. Why don't you paint one of your own?"

This young girl looked at him with troubled eyes. "But, Daddy," she said, "Miss Ellis doesn't like my kind of painting." She held up a sheet of paper with a pale purple, dittoed triangle scrawled in the middle, the conventional shape of a sail. "Miss Ellis," she said with a little sigh, "wants us to make a sailboat out of this."

*You don't have to be a great artist, however,
to be faced with a decision of whether or not to take a
huge risk and color outside the lines,
or make the sky green instead of blue.*

THE CREATIVE NUDGE

How many times have we been held back from really letting go because of our own or someone else's preconception about how something should be, or look, or even feel? How often have we been forced to follow a joyless set of rules by someone who had no concept of true freedom?

Many of the masterpieces and movements in art—like the abstractions of Matisse and Picasso, or Impressionism—have come into being when a school of artists challenged the rules of what art should be. You don't have to be a great artist, however, to be faced with a decision of whether or not to take a huge risk and color outside the lines, or make the sky green instead of blue. Our own perfectionism, that deeply rooted desire to please others, often holds us captive to preconceived notions and extinguishes our creative energy.

Did James Smith's little girl find the courage to keep painting the way she liked, or did she fall victim to her teacher's command to draw her sailboat after an established pattern? We don't know, but we can hope that her unimaginative art assignment didn't rob her of knowing the joy that she'd felt that day in the meadow.

I see a strong relationship between the creative process and the ability to continue moving down life's river. Someone has defined creativity as riding the crest of the wave, while also being willing to make the most of the muck. We've all been mired in the mud of life from time to time, getting dirty, feeling tired and angry. The problem isn't that we get so miserably mired; it's that we choose to stay that way. We remain stuck in those hopeless feelings, resigned to our situation—until something or someone else nudges us to find a creative way out.

I see a strong relationship between the creative process and the ability to continue moving down life's river. Someone has defined creativity as riding the crest of the wave, while also being willing to make the most of the muck.

One purpose of this book is to lure us ditch-dwellers back onto the open road where the wind roams free, to give ourselves permission to change and grow once again. That is one hallmark of the creative person: the one who can self-start and move on. Life itself is a creative process at its best. When we live fully, then we live creatively. We discover how to pierce the mundane and find the marvelous, while we also learn how not to be so starstruck by what's marvelous that we lose sight of what it means to be in the world.

The Christian's call is to be "in the world and yet not of it," an apt description of the stance creative souls need to take in life. God says, "Behold! I make all things new." Life is a richly creative process in which all God's children are called to participate, for creativity is nothing less than the making of the new, or the arranging of the old in new and fresh ways.

Just in case you might think I am exempting myself from this dynamic, let me tell you another episode in my life. Over ten years ago, I received a number of letters from an editor at Harper and Row in the San Francisco office named Roy Carlisle. He had heard about my ministry and research with adult singles, and wanted to discuss the possibility of my writing a book about my experiences. As a professional educator, I was comfortable with public speaking, but the thought of writing books absolutely intimidated me.

I did what so many of us do when something frightens us: I pretended it wasn't there. I ignored Roy's letters, preferring to remain stuck with my self-imposed limitations than explore a new opportunity. Then I traveled to a family life conference in Colorado. In the front row of the seminar which I was leading sat Roy. I felt an instant rapport, along with an intuitive sense that he would listen to me and could help me transform my insecurity about the process of writing. Hardly believing myself, I agreed to talk with him about writing a book.

After Roy and I spent hours brainstorming, what emerged was not a book about singles ministry. Instead, I began to share the story of how I came to adopt my son. Before this saga could become published, I had to deal with a loud "inner critic," a voice inside me that kept saying, "You can't write." It was the same voice that I heard when I first took entrance exams for college, the one that said, "You're too dumb."

Roy understood. "Carolyn," he said at the outset, "don't worry. I want to teach you *how* to write a book." He kept his promise and walked me through it, guiding me through the intricacies of the writing process, helping me to conceptualize chapters and sections. The published book was entitled *Tony: Our Journey Together*, the first of several books that have enabled me to offer my experience to others.

I believe that Roy entered my life at God's direction. He bolstered my confidence and helped me to glimpse a creative way to be set free from my fears and insecurities. Roy's patience and interest brought me to a place where I could share my rich experiences with readers everywhere.

Over the ten years and more that Roy and I have been friends, I've watched him take major risks for change in his own life. He had been nationally respected in the Christian publishing industry, having edited and published many major authors. With everyone, he exhibited the qualities that drew us close as friends and colleagues: an incredible listening ear when encountering anxieties and insecurities, along with the ability to bring insights and new perspectives. Simply put, this gifted man helped me understand why I did what I did.

Eventually Roy edited and published many books that dealt with the issues of abuse, spirituality, and personal recovery. He had also turned to face his own pain as an adult child of an alcoholic, which meant he was able to share out of his vulnerability and humanity. Roy understood that life was interdependent, that we were all there together. In midlife, still at the top in his field, he left a secure position to start his own editorial and literary agency, where he continued to produce books that explored connections between psychology and spirituality.

Now some years later, Roy is finally pursuing a long-anticipated Master's degree in counseling psychology. He is changing and growing; he's taking risks and enjoying life. Roy could have refused to try out new ventures and instead to stick with the "tried and true," but he didn't. That's what I call being "unstuck."

WHAT'S HOLDING *YOU* BACK?

So what *is* holding you back? What keeps you from being as creative as you'd like to be, experiencing the adventure of life to the fullest? We have already considered preconceptions that pinch us into humdrum patterns—like that pale violet triangle which was supposed to contain James Smith's daughter's idea of a boat racing before the wind. Other creativity-stiflers may include:

- an overdependence on technique, which may keep us from seeing an original solution to an old problem.
- a fear of failure, which paralyzes our ability to both aim high and accept our limitations.
- and when time grows short, the temptation to force the action or jump the gun.

Competence, as author Michael Vance has suggested in his curve for learning, must eventually become unconscious. If you have to think about it, it isn't yet a part of you. In many fields such as music, art, athletics, or surgery, there is often no substitute for technique. The briefest hesitation can be disastrous to your dream, dangerous, or even fatal. I wouldn't want any surgeon working on my body who didn't know exactly where and what to cut and how to stitch me together again!

Discipline and technique are what shape our enthusiasm and imagination, thereby making it possible to do what we desire.

This need for unconscious competence explains why musicians, artists, and athletes practice, practice, practice. If you don't have the discipline to play scales until you scream, you probably are never going to master Mozart! If you aren't knowledgeable about the lost-wax method, you will never be able to design a delicate ring or forge a fine sculpture. In order to excel at their chosen sports, professional athletes must learn to run precise pass routes, swing the bat, golf club, or tennis racket the same way every time. They all train their bodies to respond gracefully and consistently.

The creative process is not synonymous with chaos. When the earth was "without form and void," the work of creation had only begun. Discipline and technique shape our enthusiasm and imagination, thereby making it possible to do what we desire. But too *much* technique can impede the free flow of our ideas. As a famous Christian writer from the last century, John Henry Newman, once wrote, "Nothing would be done at all if a man waited until he could do it so well that no one could find fault in it."

Neither is creativity limiting. Seven words kill creativity: "We have always done it this way." Sometimes it's better to forget about "proper technique" and try it your own way. Dick Fosbury discovered this principle in the 1960's, when he perfected the back-over-the-bar "Fosbury flop" and won an Olympic medal in the high jump. Mendelssohn, the great composer and pianist, once said to a student who asked him about the "correct" fingering for a difficult piano passage, "Play it with your nose, as long as it sounds right!"

InterFEARence prevents us from maintaining the balance that requires courage at both ends: to aim a little higher than we can reach, while accepting the possibility that we might fall short and have to try again.

We like the security that proven technique offers, but we must always allow ourselves freedom to explore a fresh and original approach. The worst we can do is fail! Yet fear of failure is often what keeps our expectations beyond reach.

InterFEARence prevents us from maintaining the balance that requires courage at both ends: to aim a little higher than we can reach, while accepting the possibility that we might fall short and have to try again. God asks each of us to take precisely this risk in order to grow. God can and will do wonderful things in our lives—"the power of God, working in us will do infinitely more than we can ask or imagine." God will also allow us to learn from our failures and grow from our disappointments. Because fear robs us of both opportunity and perspective, God's love is determined to cast it out of our lives.

We block our own creativity through:

FEAR of making mistakes
FEAR of being seen as a fool
FEAR of being criticized
FEAR of being misused
FEAR of being "alone" (a person with an idea is automatically a minority of one)
FEAR of disturbing traditions and making changes
FEAR of being associated with taboos
FEAR of losing the security of habit
FEAR of losing the love of the group
FEAR of truly being an individual
—Don Koberg and Jim Bagnall
The All New Universal Travel Guide

When our efforts at creativity become frustrating, we human beings have a tendency to force the action. Have you ever worked on something delicate, like an intricate piece of machinery or a complex dress pattern, and found that you had a piece or two that wouldn't quite fit? The temptation is to force it, especially if you're pressed for time. It's always a mistake. If a part or fine element doesn't slip smoothly into place (assuming you're assembling the design in the right sequence), it's just that you haven't found the proper way of setting it there. Take a deep breath and proceed SLOWLY.

Sometimes it's not just a small piece of a puzzle, but the whole plan that won't fit. Just like winter tomatoes which have little taste, plans that are pinched and pushed and forced into place never quite achieve what we expect.

A similar phenomenon to forcing the action is jumping the gun. Have you been responsible for leading a group and rushed to evaluate your performance or the progress of the group, rather than wait to allow the group itself to reflect on their experience? The result of being prematurely anxious for affirmation or results is like eating a half-baked cookie.

Creative change requires time. It's important to let ideas incubate, to allow an activity to finish, to permit the mind to form around experience. Time has a fullness, and it is always wise to let the proper moment arrive. A few years ago, Orson Welles intoned a phrase that made a lot of money for a wine company: "We sell no wine before its time." That advice applies to much more than just wine.

A MATTER OF HEART

Sometimes our thinking can become polarized in a way that inhibits freedom and creativity. We may judge the finish solely on the basis of the start or lose the ability to compromise when things don't go exactly as planned. Strategy and ability count for a lot, whatever we try in life. But just as frequently, success becomes a matter of heart.

Perhaps you remember the inspirational scene in the movie *Chariots of Fire*, where the hero, an evangelist and athlete, runs the quarter mile against his stiffest competition. While a prominent coach looks on, he trips and falls in the first hundred yards. All the runners pass him by, but this determined Scotsman wills himself to get up, charges from the back of the pack into the lead, and takes the race just at the tape.

Creativity, like life, is hard work. It requires that we be alert to changing patterns, or when we can't change them, that we be open to their rearrangement. Most of us have seen the portrait which from one point of view looks like a beautiful woman from the Moulin Rouge, but which suddenly becomes that of an ugly crone when you allow your mind and eye to see its elements differently. Switching back and forth between both perspectives requires a flexible eye, open to other points of view, new possibilities and unexpected outcomes.

So often, we use our creativity to invent excuses for ourselves, to postpone even the possibility of new healing in favor of clinging to familiar things. Familiar settings give us all a feeling of security. We often strive for that kind of familiarity in our emotions, in our careers, in our relationships, in every aspect of our lives. We may not like where we are—hurting, lonely, unhappy, perhaps even bored—but at least we know those feelings and have developed coping mechanisms to help us bear them.

Creativity, like life, is hard work.

We can rationalize that we're unhappy with our jobs by saying to ourselves, "Well, that's why they call it *work!*" So many individuals resign themselves to their pain. They move along haltingly on their journey, wincing with every step, like someone who limps to keep weight off a bum knee that he's afraid to let a doctor examine. Thousands of families have learned not only how to keep silent about the pain that remains unresolved in their family structure but also how to make allowances for that pain as if it were supposed to be part of their lives.

That kind of persistent denial cannot always be overcome alone. All great spiritual teachers know that this is where we must turn to God. Thomas Merton, the wise Roman Catholic monastic and celebrated author, put it this way: "Real self-conquest is the conquest of ourselves, not by ourselves, but by the Holy Spirit. We have to have enough mastery of ourselves to renounce our own will into the hands of Christ, so that he may conquer what we cannot reach by our own efforts."

God promises that Christ will be at work within us to make us whole, or that he will work through another person close to us. The important thing is to recognize God's illuminative action when he offers that light for our creative spirit.

Jesus spoke often of our need for *repentance—metanoia* is the Greek word for it in the oldest gospel texts. It means a turning from an old life toward the promise of new life with God. Jesus found that people were not always ready for such a radical change. They held back and made excuses, some of them very plausible. "Not just yet Lord, I have to say goodbye to my mother and my father.... I have a funeral to attend... I've got a little too much responsibility to give everything up right at this moment. You understand... don't you?"

When I speak to audiences on the subject of change, I often ask them, "If Jesus were to walk up to you in a time of personal depression or frustration and ask you if you really wanted to be healed, to grow, to change, what would your answer be?" Would your reply begin with one of these phrases?

- "I'd love to, but I'm not sure you understand my problem."
- "It's just not fair that I'm the one who has to change!"
- "I know I'm hurting, but I can't help it."
- "I would have changed long ago, if only _____ wouldn't have happened." (You fill in the blank.)
- "I just can't live without _____."
  (Again, you supply the ending.)
- "I don't know if I've got enough money to take that risk. What if I lose my job, my house, my car, my nice clothes?"

In order to pursue our hopes and dreams, we have to face our own future with courage and invite change.

Maybe you would be too polite to say what you were feeling out loud, but you'd be thinking, "I can't give up my favorite crutch. I'll fall on my face! Anyway, maybe it's easier just to stay right here." When we examine these answers, we realize that what really holds us back is nothing more or less than ourselves.

In order to pursue our hopes and dreams, we have to face our own future with courage and invite change. Hindsight is always easier, but sooner or later it comes time to look ahead. We must ask ourselves, "Where are we going? Where will we be a year from now? Will we be essentially the same, or will God have brought change into our lives? Do we really want God to do that, or would we prefer to hold on to what we have and who we are? Are we really willing to break free and become unstuck?"

One year from today, I don't want to be the same person I am now. It's not that I'm unhappy with who I am now, but I do want to move ahead in my life's journey. God has adventures for me that call me forward, and I can't stay in my present spot too long, however comfortable I might be.

What's true for me is true for each one of us. God is calling you to break free and receive life, one that holds incredible adventures and experiences. The choice is yours to make. If we want to move on, to savor that new life, to achieve a new plateau, then we can't hold on or even look back for long. God calls us to venture out into the current and let him empower us, like the Star Trek crew, "to boldly go where we've never gone before."

When you do choose to break free, you'll be guaranteed an amazing journey, full of new experiences you never could have anticipated. Since healing is an ongoing process, you'll have to pause and look back from time to time to regain your strength and continue the journey. However, once it's time to move on again, here are five simple rules to keep in mind:

1. In order to move on, you have to let go.
2. You have to be willing to take the first step.
3. Rather than dwell on your weaknesses, you need to find your strengths.
4. Accept the risk of being criticized.
5. Get ready to discover a whole new you!

RULE NUMBER ONE: LEARN TO LET GO

Have you ever packed too much for a vacation and found that you had to carry unnecessary luggage around for weeks? You stuffed the trunk of your car with extra changes of clothes, a few books you "had to read," work you thought you might get to, food for on-the-road snacks, equipment for every conceivable emergency, maps in case you got lost, appliances, cosmetics, even treats for the dog! You didn't feel ready to leave until you had all that precious stuff stowed away. Sometimes the load seems so heavy that you didn't think you could make the trip until you got a bigger car to hold all the things you couldn't leave behind.

Part of being human means that we carry around baggage that we are reluctant to jettison. That unnecessary luggage then accompanies us throughout our journey and sometimes can keep us even from getting started. It is said that the longest journey begins with a single step. I believe that's true. But before we can take that first step, we have to open our hands and drop whatever is holding us back.

In order to move on, you have to be willing to let go, even of what you think you can't possibly do without. We cling to stuff that's become familiar, simply because we've dealt with it for years. Sure, some of it causes us pain, but somehow we find that safer and easier to bear than the unsettling prospect of letting it go. Old habits are hard to break, especially after they have progressed into deep, "hard-wired" patterns. Perhaps you've heard it said that addictions are only habits that you can't seem to forsake. The clear sign of being enslaved by something is finding ourselves repeating over and over again that empty resolution, "I'll quit—tomorrow."

In order to move on, you have to be willing to let go, even of what you think you can't possibly do without.

Other patterns are equally difficult to let go. Examples might include the dysfunctional relationship that either reinforces our dependency or feeds our neediness, the bad attitude that keeps the world at bay, the secret that we can't divulge to anyone—even to God. All kinds of things keep us from moving forward. We end up making excuses and developing attitudes that keep us from having to recognize how desperately we're clutching these destructive patterns.

Unless we let go of what holds and immobilizes us, we may never feel life's adventure and never fully experience God's plan for us. God knows when it is critical for us to move on. His love is so urgent at times that in order to set us free, he will pull from our clenched hands what we ourselves can't relinquish. Like ripping adhesive tape from an old wound or yanking out a rotten tooth, it can be a painful experience.

When God has acted in my life in this way, it has taken my breath away and caused a sobbing feeling suddenly to well up from deep within my being. Recognizing God's profound love and mercy has enabled me to take a deep breath and receive grace to move. I feel like I've been splashed in the face with the ice cold water of reality, which helps me open my eyes wide to the truth of my condition. Along with this recognition always comes the grace to let go.

RULE NUMBER TWO: TAKE THE FIRST STEP

Most conferences at which I speak take place in large rooms with many doors. Once the group has gathered, the doors are closed to shut out distractions. Talk about a captive audience! As I look around the room and see those closed doors, I sometimes think that this is the way some people see life—as if they're standing in the middle of a large room with no way out.

Contrast this view to that of contestants on a quiz show who know that prizes are hidden behind the doors. Everyone can't wait to see what's behind door number one, door number two, and door number three. Will the grand prize be awarded this time around? Every member of the audience would love to rush onto the stage and open the doors themselves! There's certainly no lack of willingness to take the first step.

We often stand at the threshold of adventure in our own lives. If we will only take that first step and move toward a door that apparently is closed, we may find that in reality it is just ready to open for us. Sometimes I feel like the fortunate prince who chances upon an impenetrable hedge of thorns, only to see it melt away at the first slash of my sword. And inside the long-hidden castle where everyone has been sleeping for a hundred years lies my most cherished dream, just as Sleeping Beauty lay waiting for the prince.

Fear often keeps us from taking that first bold step, especially toward something we had once abandoned. Perhaps it means going back to school to finish our degree, or responding to a new job offer in a field where we've always felt unqualified, or breaking out of the cocoon of home and family. Leaving safe surroundings for a new city, a different profession, or a new direction can certainly be intimidating. Old tapes start to play in our heads, ones that whisper, "You're not good enough; you're not smart enough; stay with what you know." The accumulated pain of our past surfaces again, to remind us of how hard life can be.

We often stand at the threshold of adventure, if we will only take that first step.

Pain and fear conspire to keep us from taking that all-important first step. God promises to take us by the hand, to move us through the pain, and to cast out the fear. He will guide us in the journey ahead and show us wondrous tributaries that are part of the stream of life, so that we can rejoice in the adventure of it all.

However, in order to reach for God's hand, our own hand must first be open. Then we have to be willing to take the first step, and the first step is always the hardest. Once we let go of what's secure, we are forced to call upon parts of our minds and hearts that have grown rusty through disuse, like muscles that are sore when you first start to exercise. We feel unfamiliar emotions, disturbing anxieties. A little dialogue bubbles up inside us—our questions, God's answers:

- "How do I know you'll catch me, Lord?"
  "I will take you by the hand."
- "Dear God, I'm so hurt and so afraid."
  "Fear not, trust in me, take that step."
- "Heavenly Father, I don't know the way. Where will I go?"
  "Let not your heart be troubled. I will take care of you and guide you safely."

Have you felt the resistance caused by pain and fear? Have you ever asked God those kinds of questions? You may know that first step by any number of names—making a leap of faith, beginning your walk with Jesus, trusting in God, even simply taking a risk. Whatever you may call it, it's absolutely crucial for your ability to get unstuck and move on.

That step could involve finding a new job, moving to a different city, trying out for a role in your civic theater. It may sound strange, but some people are prevented from taking their first step because of a misunderstanding about God's will. It's as if they're waiting for a bolt of lightning to zap them before they'll start moving. "I can't move just yet," they may say. "I've first got to pray and fast and know God's will."

God's will for us is to have abundant life, to walk in humility with him. It's important to pray, and good to fast, but neither substitutes for putting one foot in front of the other, which is what you have to do to walk with God. You might not believe it, but you can pray, fast, and walk all at the same time! As we draw closer to the future God holds in store for each of us by combining these activities, more of God's will reveals itself.

In a way, life is just a series of first steps. The real question is, who's planning the route? Things don't always work out the way we planned, which may stop us in our tracks or even cause us to backpedal to a spot of relative safety. We may try a new idea, only to find it unsuccessful. We apply to a college or submit our short story to a publisher, but we're rejected. We place great expectations on a relationship, but it doesn't work out. Then what do we do?

Robert Burns once said that "the best laid plans of mice and men go oft awry." I can't speak for the mice, but when something happens to upset my best-laid plans, my first reaction is to stop and say, "OK, from now on, I'm not budging another inch!"

When doors close, when our plans don't work out, it is often God's way of nudging us toward something better, something closer to his plan for our lives. Because rejection and disappointment hurt, it's easy to stop moving and nurse the pain. The next time a door slams shut, try this: pivot, take one step to the right or left (your choice), and *keep moving*. Rather than backpedal, see it as an opportunity to take *another* first step. You may be surprised at where it may lead you!

I remember a time when I shut my own door, only to have it open again in a totally unexpected way. Before I wrote the book about Tony, several publishers had approached me about it. As I mentioned, the prospect of writing a book was too fearful for me. Before I entered college, I'd only been able to acquire an eighth-grade competence in reading and writing skills. Education had been so devalued by our home life, and interrupted so much by moving, that I had to spend the first two years of my college career in remedial courses.

Those courses had brought me up to speed, but had also activated some tapes in my head that told me repeatedly that I wasn't smart enough or skilled enough to write. I always thought that the fact I was a university professor merely proved God's sense of humor! My painful past became transformed into a present fear, which stopped me from taking that crucial first step.

Not knowing how to overcome my fear, I made a bargain with God that I thought would keep the subject of writing a book from ever coming up again. Since the book was the story of both me and my son, I threw out a "spiritual fleece" in prayer: *Tony* would have to tell me when it was time to write. Of course, Tony didn't know about my pact with God, nor was I about to mention it.

Two years went by, during which time I stayed securely stuck. My heels were firmly planted in the sand, and I wasn't about to be budged. Then one fine day Tony came into the kitchen, threw his arms around me, and gave me a big hug. Now, I wasn't fooled—I knew he wanted money! He did, but he also said something that caused a strange thrill to run through me. "Mom," he said, "we're doing OK now, aren't we?"

"Yes, we are," I said, because it was true.

"Well," Tony said, "I guess you can write that book now!"

Lightning had struck! And I hadn't so much as mentioned the book in two years! God was calling in the promise, rolling up the fleece. Now it was time to master my fears and take the first hesitant step toward authorship, all the while reaching for God's hand.

RULE NUMBER THREE: FIND YOUR STRENGTH

God's decision to hold me to my bargain also led me to discover the third necessity for moving on. After signing a contract, I sailed through the first steps of writing my book, which played to one of my strong suits—organization. I gathered a mountain of information for the story of Tony's adoption and our life together. Quotations, descriptions, narrative details, and facts quickly filled a huge stack of five-by-eight cards. I arranged them in historical order and organized the main themes of the book into a fifty-four-page annotated outline. This masterpiece of literary organization made me a publisher's darling overnight.

Then it was time to write.

This literary genius couldn't get a word on paper! I blocked out three days, went into my study, pulled out the outline for chapter one, and proceeded to stare blankly at my typewriter. I couldn't decide how or where to start. A strange anxiety came over me, a feeling I didn't like. I concluded it was because my house needed cleaning and spent three days scrubbing it spotless.

Once again I sat down at my typewriter; still nothing came. I buried myself in unfinished university projects, figuring that they must be distracting me from my task. I finished them all, but still couldn't write a sentence of the book. My editor, Roy, continued to believe in me but I could tell there was pressure on him to help me get unstuck.

The only thing I was good at finding were distractions. I kept putting off the writing for months, and suddenly I was no longer a hero with my publisher. "Carolyn, we need your chapter, you're two weeks... one month... two months late." I was beginning to wonder if you could be arrested for not living up to a publisher's contract!

There was one last act to this paralyzing drama. I went on a ten-day teaching mission for missionary pastors serving in the jungles of New Guinea—requiring twenty-six hours of idle flight time each way and only four hours of daily teaching on site. The rest of the days and evenings I'd be sequestered in my remote jungle "guest quarters." New Guinea is still a fairly primitive place—head hunting's only been recently banned! It's not wise to walk around much at night. I knew this, so I'd brought a battery-operated typewriter with me, with a brave resolution to finish five chapters. I didn't write one word.

I began to despair, thinking how foolish I'd been to sign a contract, and how doubly foolish to have told everybody! Paralyzed now by panic, I had a conversation with my friend Jim Conway, author of several excellent books about life stages, especially midlife crisis. What he said removed my writer's block, which by that time was about the size of Gibraltar.

"Carolyn," he said, "I know you think you can't write. We all know you can, but you've convinced yourself otherwise." Then he offered a very simple, yet profound statement. "Quit dwelling on the weaknesses you think you see, and *find your strength!* What's your communication *modus operandi?* It's obvious—you're a talker! You're a verbal communicator. Don't try to write your book. Tell it instead."

The proverbial lightbulb had switched on in my head. *Telling a book!* What a concept! Roy agreed that this was just the right solution that I had needed to get moving. I went out and bought twenty-five tape cassettes, stashed my typewriter in the garage where I couldn't see it, and proceeded to pour out the story of my journey with Tony. I told it with ease and enthusiasm; chapter by chapter, our adventure together came alive. After my secretary transcribed the tapes, I worked along with others to tighten and refine the prose. Before long, a book had taken shape. When I'd been most fearful of having hit a wall, I had suddenly found my strength.

In the process, I also began to erase some internal tapes, voiceloops of those inner critics who kept reminding me how slow I'd been at school, how inadequate I was to express my story in print. These were the tapes that even logic and professional success had failed to destroy, that three graduate degrees and doctoral study had not been able to wipe clean. They had continued to serve as stumbling blocks for faith in myself and even complete trust in God.

A witty editor once said that writer's cramp is "an affliction that attacks some writers between the ears." My own gray matter had been constricted by those grumpy, fault-finding tapes—until I was shown a way to turn down the volume and begin the erasing process. Once I'd done that, I became, in Warren Schmidt's words, a Pursuer of the Possible, not content to rest in my weakness, but willing to discover and test my strength.

When your inner critics assemble,
remember that every gift you know you possess
flowered because you believed you were worthy of it.

Part of your journey will likely involve confronting the inner voices which hold you back and keep you from discovering your strength. It's not something you do just once, however. These internal tapes are renewed in your unconscious and must be confronted time and again whenever you face new possibilities that call for strengths you didn't know you had.

When your inner critics assemble, remember that every gift you know you possess flowered because you believed you were worthy of it. Every gift you're convinced you lack may well be there as well, but you'll never know it unless you can get past those demeaning voices.

What recordings are you listening to? What strengths lie hidden for you to find? Inside each one of us are strengths and potentials that we are meant to discover and use as we move down the river. Forget those self-limiting tapes! We have God's permission to move from strength to strength in this life, from glory to glory.

RULE NUMBER FOUR:
RUNNING THE RISK OF CRITICISM

As you make your way downstream, understand that some people who are stuck on the bank will inevitably throw stones at your raft. Everybody loves approval and affirmation. It feels great to be told we're wonderful. But when we plot our course in response to God's guidance, when we let Jesus set the beat of our oars, it sets us apart.

When we don't fall in line with everybody else, we may lose the approval of those who know how to judge only according to their own standards or those of the world. "What do you mean, you're going to quit your job and go back to school?" "You must be crazy to consider getting married and raising a family in these uncertain days!" "Do you really think you're up to that new job?" "What could possess you to move from your nice apartment and buy that house? Stay in your niche and you'll be a lot better off!"

The best answer to your critics is, "I know I am where God wants me to be." Leave it up to God whether or not they'll have ears to hear it. Scripture says, "Do not conform any longer to the pattern of this world, but be transformed by the renewing of your mind..." (Rom 12:2). Every one of us who makes a decision to move on down the river comes to heed that advice firsthand.

Before you think that I'm advocating a lifestyle based on individualism run wild, I should say that it's also important to be open to criticism, because it may contain warnings God intends for us to notice and heed. In my own life, there have been several times when a single, questioning, "still, small voice" was God's way of calling me to draw closer to the right path. The most dramatic example happened to me when I was seeking a way out of the discomfort of having to take those remedial reading courses at California State Long Beach. Like most young people of age nineteen or so, I desperately wanted approval for my accomplishments, not reminders of how deficient I was.

I decided that God was calling me to go on mission to Mexico (it turned out he was, but not just yet!). I convinced myself and my church that this was my true vocation. I remember speaking on a Sunday night before a congregation of fifteen hundred people, and afterwards hearing their words of encouragement and promises of financial help. One voice, that of Jean Fonner, asked a discreet, deceptively simple question. "Carolyn," she asked, "are you sure you're not running from something?" I didn't have an answer, and somehow the impact of her question stopped me from framing a "smart-aleck" reply.

Jean quietly pressed her advantage. "Have you ever considered attending a Christian college for a while, before Mexico?" she said. "You're a new Christian, and the education you'd get would prepare you for what God's calling you to do." Her suggestion caused me to give my plans a second thought. I spent some time in concentrated prayer about my decision. God's voice, along with Jean Fonner's, carried more weight than all the approving voices of the congregation.

With some reluctance, I went to see my pastor and told him that I'd been praying! I felt I had to apologize for what I'd say next. I knew a reversal of mind would seem strange after what had happened that Sunday night. However, there was no doubt that I'd come to believe a Christian college would better prepare me for mission, to Mexico or anywhere, and I had to be honest about it. I'd changed my mind, at least for now, and I told my pastor so.

Tears welled up in his eyes as he exclaimed, "Oh, Carolyn! I thank God for that decision and for you! How can I help?" From that point, I was only a step from Azusa Pacific, which made an exception in their admissions policies to let untutored me enter a course of study there. Jean Fonner's discerning counsel had turned me in a direction that would change my life forever.

In my own journey, I have made many big decisions which have prompted some unexpected responses. At the time I decided to go to seminary to pursue another advanced degree in religious education, I was teaching in the Division of Religion and Philosophy at APU, a department where I was the only woman professor among some fifteen male faculty members. Assuming a seminary degree would make me a better teacher, I thought my colleagues would say, "Great! Go for it!" I was shocked to discover that most of them didn't approve.

"Carolyn, you do not want to go to seminary," they all said, emphatically. Was it that I might lose enthusiasm, or that I would intellectualize my Christian faith? No! They thought that no one would want to marry a woman with a seminary degree! I was concerned about my abilities as an educator. I wanted to be the best Christian education professor I could be, while they were concerned about my marital status!

The fact that Talbot Seminary at that time had a male-to-female ratio of about forty to one apparently didn't enter their heads. Their well-intentioned advice didn't fit with the times or my own current circumstances, and it frustrated me that they couldn't embrace my point of view. I went anyway and found the four-year experience all that I'd hoped it would be. God blessed my ministry richly for taking the risk.

After having lived in university housing for twelve years, I received a similar reaction when I bought a house off campus. This time it came not only from some faculty members (who seemed vaguely disturbed at this show of independence) but also from the bank. I bought my house at a time when single females were not supposed to do such a thing. We were supposed to rent and wait. The loan officer wrote "SINGLE FEMALE" in capitals with a red pen, and then underlined it a couple times for emphasis. The loan went through anyway and I got the house, which caused some of my friends to say that I'd driven another nail into my matrimonial coffin.

You can imagine the reactions when I enrolled for a Ph.D. and when I adopted Tony from the iron fist of the Mexican prison system. In a sense, they were right. Every one of these steps removed me a little further from the mainstream of eligible single women. If I were to believe some recent societal studies, I'd have more chance statistically of being atomized by a terrorist's bomb than walking down the aisle and tying the knot!

Of course, that's not really the point. If it's true that a woman lessens her chances for marriage because she's too educated, or independent, or a single parent, or because (heaven forbid!) she owns her own home, then I believe there's something wrong with the institution of matrimony. Yet in order to follow what I believed to be God's plan for me, I had to brave the opinions of narrower minds who thought my B.A. was education enough, that buying a house was inappropriate for someone who expected to be made secure by marriage, and that parenthood was strictly for Ozzie and Harriet.

I believe these decisions were intended by God in order to enrich my life adventure. In fact, these experiences were reserved for me in my stretch of the river—free for the taking. I know I am where God wants me, and always will be, despite what my critics might say.

God alone knows your heart and your capabilities. He has a custom-made plan for you, too, one that will draw you into Christian maturity and let you grow. You don't need to look exactly like everyone else. I believe God wants people to be individuals as they move down the river. It's your adventure. Don't worry about what others may say about your choice to change and grow for the better.

To change is to run the risk of self-discovery.

RULE NUMBER FIVE: ACCEPT A WHOLE NEW YOU

Drag out your high school graduation picture, blow the dust off, and take a good look. Chances are that you'll see significant differences in your appearance, but the changes aren't all on the surface. You've changed inside, too.

I am far different from Carolyn Koons, the high school senior, who peers out from the yearbook uncertain about how to face the world. I am now a professor of thirty years' standing with credentials that I couldn't have dreamed possible when I was eighteen. I speak in public with an ease that I would have found impossible to conceive. I am a good parent, by free choice and against all odds, having come from a home environment with no parental models, and where my parents' love was all but non-existent. On top of all that, I've found a way to share my story which helps people face change and challenge in their own lives. God has brought out gifts from me that have changed my life completely, inside and out, from that time when I stood on the threshold of adulthood. My walk with God has grown more exciting year by year, and for that I rejoice, with all my heart.

To change is to run the risk of self-discovery. Some of that discovery may be good—hidden talents and strengths are always fun to learn about. Other discoveries may be less thrilling, when we find out about traits we don't like.

I remember when I asked ten of my teaching colleagues to evaluate me and my work. I invited them to put me under the microscope after having gone through the most exhausting and challenging years of my life. I'd spent an enormous amount of energy in the adoption process with Tony, and megawatts more in learning how to be an effective parent. I truly wondered what I had going for me after all that I'd been through. I knew how I saw myself, but was also aware that my insights were neither objective nor crystal clear.

I didn't have the strength for a rigorous self-evaluation, but it was still quite another thing to invite people to share how they saw me. If they were honest with me, they'd certainly come up with both strengths and weaknesses I never knew were there. I decided to accept whatever I found out, and not to deny it. That way, I could look at areas where I needed improvement and develop a definite plan for change.

In the end, my friends were honest and fair, and I was glad that I asked them for their input. Because I didn't waste time and energy (I had precious little of either) defending the "old me," I found that I was ready to welcome a new person—one who could still grow because she was willing to change.

Be prepared to grow by getting to know that new person who's ready to step out and shake hands with the world. Be willing to "go outside the dotted lines" to find that new person. Let your margins leak a little! Change means renewal, a tapping of new energy, a better sense of where you're going and how you'll get there. God is building a wonderful life for that new you. All you have to do is be willing to take the risk.

Having seen how change can take many forms in our lives, we need to ask two questions in order to see just how we're changing: Have we broken free? Are we soaring, or are we still stuck?

Two more questions then open up, the answers to which will differ from person to person: Have we let go of those things that weigh us down and keep us from moving on? Have we found the courage to take that first step, to concentrate on our strengths, to silence the voices of our critics—both inside and out? If we can answer yes to these, then we are well on our way to becoming a living fulfillment of God's promise, "Behold, I am making all things new."

Be prepared to grow by getting to know that new person who's ready to step out and shake hands with the world.

I once came across an inspirational poetic message which describes that new person well. The author may have intended to portray God's wish for his beloved children on their journey. I've adapted it a little to capture the feeling of God speaking directly to each of us. It's called "Do What You've Never Done Before":

Do what you've never done before,
see what you've never seen,
feel what you've never felt,
say what you've never said.
Bear what you've never borne,
and hear what you've never heard.

All is not what it would seem,
nothing ever remains the same.
Change is life's characteristic,
so bend and flow, and play the game.

So many times you were the one
who stopped yourself from doing things.
So many times you grounded yourself,
clipped your own wings.

So I say to you:
Do what you've never done before,
and go where you have never been.

This new person—the "new you"—is blessed with a sense of adventure, a desire to go down the river, to travel light, to brave the potholes and haystacks of white water, to avoid the pitfalls that seek to ensnare us, to lighten the burden of pain, and to welcome the changes that will bring freedom. The new you is unstuck, not just coping with change in adult life, but thriving on a diet of new experience and healthy growth, all made possible by God's love. So let it be in your own life, in Jesus' name. Amen.

BIBLIOGRAPHY

Bradshaw, John. *Homecoming: Reclaiming and Championing Your Inner Child* (New York, New York: Bantam, 1988). In my opinion, the best of Bradshaw's work.... It's important, however, to do some serious and honest reflection before applying his insights to your life. They go down so easily that you tend to swallow them whole, rather than do the necessary work to make it true for *you.*

Conway, Jim. *Adult Children of Legal or Emotional Divorce: Healing Your Long-Term Hurt* (Downers Grove, Illinois: InterVarsity Press, 1990). Becoming the healthy, whole person you want to be may be very painful at times, but Conway says; "Let's make the decision to be healed. Let's cut off the tentacles from the past that are squeezing the life out of us. Let's expect wholeness for ourselves and for all the people important to us."

Covey, Stephen R. *The Seven Habits of Highly Effective People: Restoring the Character Ethic* (New York, New York: Simon & Schuster Inc., 1989). With penetrating insights and pointed anecdotes, Covey reveals a step-by-step pathway for living with fairness, integrity, honesty, and human dignity—principles that give us the security to adapt to change, and the wisdom and power to take advantage of the opportunities that change creates.

Crabb, Larry. *Inside Out* (Colorado Springs, Colorado: NavPress, 1988). Real change may not be what you think it is. It has everything to do with facing the realities of your own internal life and letting God mold you into a person who is free to be honest, courageous, and loving. "Only Christians have the capacity to never pretend about anything," says Larry Crabb.

213

Dickson, Elaine. *Say No, Say Yes to Change* (Nashville, Tennessee: Broadman Press, 1982). There couldn't be life as we know it without change. Still, change makes us fearful as well as hopeful, sad as well as joyful. Those who truly live come to terms with change—make friends with it. A real friend is someone you can say yes and no to. So making friends with change involves saying both yes and no and knowing which is appropriate.

Foster, Richard J. *Celebration of Discipline: The Path to Spiritual Growth,* revised edition (San Francisco, California: Harper-Collins, 1988). An excellent guide to the twelve inward, outward, and corporate disciplines of the spiritual life. Clearly written, with timeless practical guidance.

Halpern, Howard M. *Cutting Loose: An Adult Guide to Coming to Terms With Your Parents* (New York, New York: Bantam Books, 1983). How to be yourself—not your parent's child. In this book, psychotherapist Howard Halpern describes how people get stuck in frustrating parent/child patterns and how to get out of them. He shows how you can break the old routines and begin to enjoy better, happier relations with your parents—as adults, as equals, even as friends.

Hart, Archibald D. *Healing Life's Hidden Addictions: Overcoming the Closet Compulsions that Waste Your Time and Control Your Life* (Ann Arbor, Michigan: Servant Publications, 1990). In addition to offering sound medical and psychological insight, Hart probes deeply into the spiritual dynamic at the heart of addiction and points to the path of grace. This book helps you determine whether you are at risk for a hidden addiction. More than that, it offers help to anyone who wants to find a way out of hidden addictions, for themselves or someone they care about.

Kanter, Elizabeth Moss. *The Change Masters: Innovation and Entrepreneurship in the American Corporation* (New York, New York: Simon & Schuster, 1983). The key to an American corporate renaissance, says Kanter, lies in innovation, entrepreneurship, and the development of "participative management" skills that encourage the use of new ideas arising from within the corporation itself.

Keillor, Garrison. *We Are Still Married,* (New York, New York: Viking, 1989).

Kidd, Sue Monk. *When the Heart Waits: Spiritual Direction for Life's Sacred Questions* (San Francisco, California: Harper-Collins, 1990). Some books take courage to read, because they take us to places within our own soul that we avoid, places wherein God dwells, places where it takes time to go. This beautifully written and narrated book is one of those.

Kirkpatrick, Donald L. *How To Manage Change Effectively* (San Francisco, California: Jossey-Bass Publishers, 1985). A helpful professional book on this difficult subject.

Koberg, Dan and Jim Bagnall. *The Revised All New Universal Traveler,* (Los Altos, California: William Kaufman, 1981). Koberg and Bagnall are teachers of design at California Polytechnic San Luis Obispo. Their book is an original, often wise, frequently funny approach to solving problems creatively while on life's journey.

Koons, Carolyn. *Tony: Our Journey Together.* (San Francisco, California: Harper-Collins, 1984). *Beyond Betrayal: Healing My Broken Past* (San Francisco, California: HarperCollins, 1986).

Manning, Brennan. *The Ragamuffin Gospel: Good News for the Bedraggled, Beat-Up, and Burnt Out* (Portland, Oregon: Multnomah, 1990). If you've tried to appease God by being special enough, if you've tried to please God by being good enough, if you've tried to satisfy God by being pure enough, if you've tried to pacify God by giving enough, if you've given it your best only to find your best is never enough, if you're bone-tired with burdens too big for your back, this book is for you.

Maxwell, Glyn. "Rumpelstilskin," *The Atlantic*, vol. 269, No. 1, (January 1992.)

Naisbitt, John. *Megatrends: Ten New Directions Transforming Our Lives* (New York, New York: Warner Books, 1982). *Megatrends* is a primer that outlines where our sophisticated technology is taking us, how we will be governed, and how America's social structures will change. It's the challenge, the means, and the method to better our lives... a must for everyone who cares about the future.

Ratliff, J. Bill. *When You Are Facing Change* (Louisville, Kentucky: Westminster/John Knox Press, 1989). Facing change in our lives does not have to be a traumatic experience. It can be a time of enlightenment. Ratliff describes the types of change one is likely to encounter in life and then tells how to deal with endings, uncertainties, and new beginnings.

Reed, Bobbie. *Learning to Risk: Finding Joy as a Single Adult* (Grand Rapids, Michigan: Zondervan Publishing House, 1990). As Reed says, the abundant life that God wishes for us is "not a prescribed set of circumstances God sets up for us, a fulfillment of all our dreams and hopes. It is, rather, an attitude of expectancy, appreciation, and confidence that God will enable us to handle all of life's circumstances, even those that might look like nightmares. The abundant life is ours for the choosing."

Schaller, Lyle E. *The Change Agent* (Nashville, Tennessee: Abingdon Press, 1982). The imperative need for social change today has made almost everyone an agent of change, in one capacity or another. Schaller advocates a systematic and anticipatory approach to planned social change. He considers all aspects of the process of change, including styles, tactics, and the nature of change, the place of power, the possible points of conflict, and the avoidance of polarization. For anyone who is striving for progress in human relations this lively and readable book provides a knowledgeable approach to the dynamics of change.

Seamands, David A. *Healing for Damaged Emotions* (Wheaton, Illinois: Victor Books, 1981). If you are hurting emotionally, this book will help you. God can break the chains from your past and free you to live. He can recycle your hang-ups into wholeness.

Sell, Charles. *Unfinished Business: Helping Adult Children Resolve Their Past* (Portland, Oregon: Multnomah, 1989). The good news is, we don't have to be enslaved to the past. Sell combines personal experience with extensive research in detailing the traits common to adult children. Without accusing or attacking, he reveals the impact of our childhood families and provides a biblically-based resolution of inner conflict.

Sine, Tom. *Wild Hope: A Rallying Call to Take Charge and Live Creatively in a Changing World* (Dallas, Texas: Word, Inc., 1991). Sine is one of the few trained futurists who understands the challenges facing the church in the years to come. He also provocatively and intelligently confronts our apathy and assumptions about the future. As Jimmy Carter says, "An important book for all people of faith."

Smalley, Gary, and John Trent. *The Blessing* (Nashville, Tennessee: Thomas Nelson Publishers, 1986). No matter your age, the approval of your parents affects how you view yourself and your ability to pass that approval along to your children, spouse, and friends. Many people spend a lifetime looking for this acceptance that the Bible calls "the blessing."

Tada, Joni Eareckson. *Choices, Changes* (Grand Rapids, Michigan: Zondervan Books, 1986). "And as I sit, I've observed with curiosity the way we Christians grasp for the future as if the present didn't quite satisfy. How we, in spiritual fits and starts, scrape and scratch our way along, often missing the best of life while looking the other way, preoccupied with shaping our future." This very personal look outlines how God has taken Joni Eareckson Tada through the changing winds of doubts and difficulties into the still, calm choice to believe and obey God.

Thurman, Howard. "How Good It Is...", Quotes in *Cathedral Age*, (Washington National Cathedral), Summer 1992.

Watzlawick, Paul, John H. Weakland and Richard Fisch. *Change: Principles of Problem Formation and Problem Resolution* (New York, New York: W.W. Norton & Company, 1974). This book deals with age-old questions of persistence and change in human affairs. More particularly, it is concerned with how problems arise and are perpetuated in some instances, and resolved in others. While the authors draw some of their examples from the field of psychotherapy, their premises regarding the formation and resolution of problems are applicable in the much wider and more general areas of human interaction, including large social systems and even international relations.

Wuellner, Flora. "Transformation: Our Fear, Our Longing," *Weavings: A Journal of the Christian Spiritual Life*, No. 2 (March/April 1991), (Nashville, Tennessee: The Upper Room).

Other Books of Interest by Servant Publications

Family Is *Still* a Great Idea
H. Norman Wright

Noted family counselor and bestselling author Norman Wright provides valuable insights into what makes these families work so well and demonstrates how we, too, can build the same kind of love and strength into relationships with our loved ones.

$14.99

Rediscovering Holiness
J.I. Packer

In *Rediscovering Holiness,* the way to personal holiness is once more clearly marked out for us, pointing to true freedom and joy.   *$16.99*

Available at your Christian bookstore or from:
**Servant Publications • Dept. 209 • P.O. Box 7455
Ann Arbor, Michigan 48107**
Please include payment plus $1.25 per book
for postage and handling.
*Send for our FREE catalog of Christian
books, music, and cassettes.*